Law Clerk Handbook

A Handbook for Law Clerks to Federal Judges

Honorable Alvin B. Rubin
U.S. Circuit Judge
U.S. Court of Appeals for the Fifth Circuit

Laura B. Bartell
Member of the New York Bar

Federal Judicial Center
Revised 1989

This publication was produced in furtherance of the Center's statutory mission to develop and conduct programs of continuing education and training for personnel of the federal judicial system. The statements, conclusions, and points of view are those of the authors. This work has been reviewed by Center staff, and publication signifies that it is regarded as responsible and valuable. It should be emphasized, however, that on matters of policy the Center speaks only through its Board.

Cite as A. Rubin & L. Bartell, Law Clerk Handbook
(Federal Judicial Center rev. ed. 1989).

ISBN 0-314-73306-X

FJC-M-89-2

Table of Contents

About the Authors

Alvin B. Rubin received his LL.B. from Louisiana State University Law School in 1942. He has served on the United States District Court for the Eastern District of Louisiana from 1966 to 1977, and since then on the U.S. Court of Appeals for the Fifth Circuit. He has been an adjunct professor of law at the Louisiana State University Law School since 1946, and is now an adjunct lecturer at Southern University Law School, an adjunct faculty member at Duke University School of Law, and a member of the Board of Editors of the *Manual for Complex Litigation, Second.* He has served as a member of the Board of the Federal Judicial Center.

Laura B. Bartell received her J.D. degree from Harvard Law School in 1978. After serving as a law clerk for Judge Rubin on the Court of Appeals for the Fifth Circuit, she entered private practice in New York City where she is a partner in the firm of Shearman & Sterling. She has been a lecturer at many continuing legal education programs sponsored by the American Law Institute–American Bar Association and has also lectured at workshops for federal judges sponsored by the Federal Judicial Center.

Preface

The partnership between a federal judge and the judge's clerk can be a splendid and mutually rewarding relationship. For a young lawyer, a clerkship for a federal judge provides an opportunity to hone research and writing skills, to gain practical familiarity with the litigation process, and to enhance the lawyer's understanding of the legal profession and the decision-making process. For the judge, clerks who understand the role they are asked to play and who perform their tasks well become personal extensions who enable the judge to perform judicial duties more efficiently. The purpose of this handbook is to help law clerks understand tasks they will be asked to undertake and to perform them more effectively.

This handbook is intended not to be dogmatic; relatively little of what it contains is indisputable. Our purpose is to offer one view of practical procedures that may assist both the clerk and the judge in working together. Other judges will have approaches that differ from those suggested here, and will wish law clerks to handle problems in the manner they consider most appropriate. Of course, the mandatory procedure for each law clerk is the one dictated by the judge for whom the clerk works.

It is not feasible to review the procedures of each district and appellate court in this handbook. Clerks should themselves make notations of local court or office procedures for their own use and for the guidance of their successors and add them either as inserts in or supplements to this handbook. Different aspects of common law clerk functions and different aspects of court operations are treated at various places of the handbook. The table of contents is therefore a guide to its effective use.

This handbook includes materials drawn from many sources, including various manuals already in use in circuit or district courts and from prior law clerks' manuals prepared for the first edition by William L. Whittaker, Esq., and by Peter B. Carey, Esq., under the direction of the Federal Judicial Center. Anthony M. DiLeo, Esq., was coauthor of the first edition of this handbook after clerking for Judge Rubin on the district court and for Judge John Minor Wisdom of the Fifth Circuit Court of Appeals.

Mr. DiLeo contributed immeasurably to this work. Bankruptcy Judge Wesley W. Steen (M.D. La.) has contributed the sections discussing the special duties of clerks to bankruptcy judges. We are grateful for his contribution. We are also grateful to the three directors of the Federal Judicial Center, Judge Walter E. Hoffman, A. Leo Levin, and Judge John Godbold, who have inspired and aided us, and to Kenneth C. Crawford, who, as a member of the Center staff, provided us continued support. We express special thanks to Dr. Russell R. Wheeler, director of the Division of Special Educational Services, who served as our counselor and editor and contributed innumerable valuable suggestions for this edition.

Alvin B. Rubin
Baton Rouge, Louisiana

Laura B. Bartell
New York, New York

CHAPTER 1. INTRODUCTION

§ 1. The Function and Role of the Law Clerk

A law clerk is a lawyer employed to assist a judge with as many administrative, clerical, and basic legal tasks as possible, so as to leave the judge more time for judging and critical decision-making. The clerk has no statutorily defined duties. Instead, the clerk carries out the judge's instructions. In doing so, the typical clerk is given a broad range of duties. Clerks are usually assigned to do legal research, prepare bench memos, draft orders and opinions, edit and proofread the judge's orders and opinions, and verify citations. Many judges discuss pending cases with their law clerks and confer with them about decisions. Frequently, clerks also maintain the library, assemble documents, serve as courtroom crier, and run errands for the judge. District court clerks also often attend conferences in chambers with the attorneys in a case.

Each judge decides cases in an individual manner and has work habits developed in a long professional career. No two judges, therefore, utilize their clerks in precisely the same manner. The law clerk must follow the instructions and adjust to the requirements and habits of the individual judge for whom the clerk works.

The judge is also assisted by other staff members. An appellate judge is authorized to employ three law clerks and two secretaries. Each district judge generally has two law clerks, a secretary, a courtroom deputy, and the services of a court reporter. Each bankruptcy judge has one law clerk and a secretary. Each magis-

1

trate has a clerical assistant and a secretary. With the approval of the Magistrate's Committee of the Judicial Conference, a magistrate may employ a law clerk instead, and the clerical assistant's position is assigned to the office of the clerk of court, which then furnishes clerical assistance to the magistrate.

As a member of the judge's staff, the clerk must work cooperatively with the other staff members so that, as a team, they assist the judge in fulfilling judicial responsibilities. Although each member of the staff has certain specific duties, the staff members assist each other.

§ 2. The Trial Court Law Clerk and the Appellate Court Law Clerk

Like their judicial principals, district court and bankruptcy court clerks perform a wider variety of functions than do appellate court clerks. The trial court is engaged in the process of fact-finding, including discovery and trial, and in the myriad details of the daily processing of litigation, including discovery disputes; settlement conferences; pretrial, trial, and post-trial motions; and sentencing in criminal cases. The bankruptcy court clerk likewise participates in the broad range of tasks performed by the bankruptcy judge as a trial judge. Trial court clerks have substantially more contact with attorneys and witnesses and are involved in the many decisions made at every stage of each case.

Most district court and bankruptcy court opinions are not published, and most need not contain an exhaustive review of the relevant precedents. A trial court opinion has limited precedential effect, ordinarily only as persuasive authority, and an opinion is published only when the trial judge elects to send it to the companies that publish federal court opinions or maintain them in on-line services. On the rare occasion when the trial judge thinks it desirable, the trial court opinion may contain an exhaustive and detailed analysis of the state of the law, much like an appellate court opinion. Appellate courts may adopt a district court opinion when affirming the district court.

In contrast, the principal function of the clerk for an appellate judge is to research the issues of law and fact presented by an appeal. The clerk may be called upon to prepare a bench memo, to assist the judge in preparing for oral argument, to prepare a draft of an opinion pursuant to the judge's directions, or to edit or cite-check an opinion written by the judge. Appellate opinions are frequently published and become precedent for all district courts in the circuit. In addition, although an appeal may be taken from any trial court final decision, and most judgments rendered after a trial on the merits or summary judgment are now appealed, the decisions of the federal circuit courts of appeals are often conclusive because the Supreme Court of the United States grants review in only a small percentage of the cases sought to be brought to it. Consequently, appellate opinions require comprehensive analysis and synthesis of the relevant existing decisions.

§ 3. The Educational Experience of the Law Clerk

A clerk learns by doing and by participating in making real decisions. The education of a clerk is pragmatic and practical. The clerk learns by association with the judge, who was formerly an accomplished practitioner or educator, and by attending trials, conferences, or oral arguments. The education is not limited to legal analysis; it includes exposure to the methods and customs of practitioners and the level of professional behavior that is expected of lawyers, as well as experience with the full range of legal styles and abilities presented in federal court. The clerk learns what to expect of others and develops personal standards of professional conduct. Clerking provides direct insight into the judicial process, a unique opportunity for those who intend to engage in litigation or teaching. The clerk's contact with this process of adjudicating disputes contributes to the development of skills in analysis and expression and to understanding the practical side of legal problem-solving.

Moreover, the clerk faces significant legal issues of the day and has the opportunity to consider the social and economic implications of deciding those issues. Observing the challenging roles that judges and lawyers play in the resolution of controversies, and contributing to that process, add to the clerk's own professional development.

§ 4. Historical Development

Although the titles and duties have varied, the position of law clerk has existed within the federal judiciary for more than a century. Justice Horace Gray, appointed to the Supreme Court of the United States in 1881, introduced to that Court his practice (originally adopted while he was Chief Justice of the Supreme Judicial Court of Massachusetts) of employing at his own expense an honor graduate of Harvard Law School as his secretary. Gray's practice was continued by his successor on the Court, Justice Oliver Wendell Holmes.

In 1885, the Attorney General of the United States, in his report to Congress, recommended that each justice of the Supreme Court be "provided by law with a secretary or law clerk . . . to assist in such clerical work as might be assigned to him." In 1886, pursuant to that recommendation, Congress provided clerical assistants to the justices. Forty-four years later, in 1930, provision was made for law clerks for U.S. circuit court judges; in 1936, for the U.S. district court judges; in 1979, for U.S. magistrates; and in 1984, for U.S. bankruptcy judges.

At present, each Supreme Court justice is authorized four law clerks (28 U.S.C. § 675); each circuit judge, three (28 U.S.C. § 712); each district judge, two (28 U.S.C. § 752); and each bankruptcy judge, two (28 U.S.C. § 156(a)). Each magistrate is authorized a clerical assistant, or, when certified, a law clerk (28 U.S.C. § 634(c), 635(a); *Judicial Conference Report,* September 1987, at 63). In addition, all appellate and some district courts are authorized to employ staff law clerks, who serve the entire court.

§ 5. Information for Applicants

The first opportunity any prospective law clerk has to learn the requirements of a particular judge is during the application process. Some judges send those seeking the position a written job description; such a summary assists applicants in gauging their interest. A summary may include the current salary, duration of the appointment, basic responsibilities of the clerk, predominant types of litigation dealt with by the court, and similar general information. A summary of this kind may shorten a personal interview and save the judge from repeating answers to common applicant questions. Sample summaries for district court and appellate court clerkships are available from the Federal Judicial Center.

Clerkship applicants should not only review any summary provided by the judge, but should also take advantage of all other opportunities to learn about the requirements of the specific job and the personal characteristics of the judge for whom they might work. Some judges encourage applicants whom they are seriously considering to discuss frankly and confidentially with their incumbent law clerks the judge's personality, temperament, and work habits so that the applicant can be assured before making a final commitment that the relationship is likely to be rewarding. Judges—even those within the same district or city—are not fungible, and both judge and clerk will find the clerkship a more pleasant experience if they find in each other the right match of interests and personality.

§ 6. Preparation for Clerking

After accepting the offer of a clerkship, the clerk-to-be should inquire whether the judge recommends that the clerk take any particular courses during the remainder of the clerk's law school career. Obviously, every clerk will benefit from courses in federal jurisdiction, federal civil procedure, evidence (including the Federal Rules of Evidence), criminal procedure, and constitutional law. In addition, the court in which the clerk will serve may have a large volume of litigation in some particular area, and each judge may believe that some special courses would be especially helpful. The clerk for a district judge should acquire a paperbound copy of the Federal Rules of Criminal Procedure, the Federal Rules of Civil Procedure, and the Federal Rules of Evidence. The clerk for a bankruptcy judge should acquire in addition a copy of the Bankruptcy Rules. The clerk for an appellate judge should also own a copy of the Federal Rules of Appellate Procedure, commonly referred to as FRAP. Although the judge will have copies of these in the library, having a personal copy for the clerk's use will help the clerk become familiar with the rules and make them available at all times. The clerk should also get a copy of the local rules of court, standing orders, and other operating procedures, and study them carefully.

Some judges, or clerks, have prepared outlines describing the judge's particular style and procedures, and even providing suggestions for the new clerk. Examples of such documents are available from the Federal Judicial Center.

In addition, the clerk should consider some background reading on the judicial process. Judge Ruggero J. Aldisert's *The Judicial Process* is a rich collection of readings and analysis. Judge Frank Coffin's *The Ways of a Judge* provides numerous insights on the decision-making process. Reading these as well as the works cited at the end of this chapter will help a prospective clerk more fully understand the judge's role and the clerk's.

The Federal Judicial Center has numerous publications dealing not only with federal court operations, but also with specific subjects such as habeas corpus, employment discrimination, Social Security appeals, immigration law, and "black lung" cases. Consult the Center's *Catalog of Publications,* which is issued annually, for specific titles. A clerk may also wish to consult the Center's annual *Catalog of Audiovisual Media Programs* for audiocassettes and videotapes of possible interest. The Center's *Bench Book for United States District Court Judges* (3d ed.) contains much specific information about case management and the judicial process in the trial court.

A clerk will want a few personal reference books, too. Each law clerk should have a dictionary, a thesaurus, a copy of *A Uniform System of Citation,* published by the Harvard Law Review Association, and the University of Chicago *Manual of Legal Citation.* It is also useful to have a style book, such as *A Manual of Style,* published by the University of Chicago Press; the *Harbrace College Handbook;* or the *Gregg Reference Manual.* Before writing the first assignment for a judge, every clerk should read Strunk and White, *The Elements of Style* (3d ed.), and then periodically reread it.

§ 7. Continuing Education for Law Clerks

Many courts provide orientation programs for law clerks and some provide various kinds of local educational programs for court personnel generally or for the bar. Newly appointed clerks should ask whether the court has any such programs and, if it does, what programs are open to them.

Although the Federal Judicial Center provides continuing education and training for judges and permanent court employees, the Board of the Center has determined, due to the temporary nature of law clerks' employment, that these Center resources cannot be made available to clerks except in unusual circumstances. Although Center funds may only rarely be expended directly on continuing education for law clerks, the Center has no objection to clerks taking advantage of Center programs at no cost to the Center. The clerk may, for example, ask the judge or the court's "training coordinator" if it is appropriate for the clerk to attend a local program. Also, Center publications (such as this handbook) and audiovisual materials are available to clerks, as noted above.

§ 8. Miscellaneous

The new clerk should become familiar with the details of employee benefits, such as health insurance, policy as to leave (paid and unpaid), and other particulars. Typically, a personnel specialist in the office of the clerk of court can explain the government-wide and judiciary-wide policies and options. On some matters, such as office hours and leave policy, the clerk should also learn the particular preferences of the judge. Some courts have other, specific practices, such as certificates of completion at the end of a clerk's term.

§ 9. Suggested Supplementary Reading

28 U.S.C. § 675 (law clerks to Supreme Court justices)

28 U.S.C. § 712 (law clerks to circuit judges)

28 U.S.C. § 752 (law clerks to district judges)

28 U.S.C. § 156(a) (law clerks to bankruptcy judges)

28 U.S.C. § 635(a) (law clerks to magistrates)

Acheson, *Recollections of Service with the Federal Supreme Court,* 18 Ala. L. Rev. 355 (1957)

Ackerman, *In Memoriam: Henry J. Friendly,* 99 Harv. L. Rev. 1709 (1986)

Aldisert, Review of Schwartz, *Super Chief: Earl Warren and His Supreme Court,* 72 Calif. L. Rev. 275 (1984)

Baier, *The Law Clerks: Profile of an Institution,* 26 Vand. L. Rev. 1125 (1973)

Braden, *The Value of Law Clerks,* 24 Miss. L.J. 295 (1953)

Brudney & Wolfson, *Mr. Justice Rutledge—Law Clerk's Reflections,* 25 Ind. L.J. 455 (1959)

Crump, *How Judges Use Their Law Clerks,* N.Y. St. B.J. 43 (May 1986)

Dorsen, *Law Clerks in Appellate Courts in the United States,* 26 Mod. L. Rev. 265 (1963).

Fite, *Law Clerkships—Three Inside Views,* 33 Ala. L. Rev. 155 (1972)

Hills, *A Law Clerk at the Supreme Court of the United States,* 33 L.A. B. Bull. 333 (1958)

Improving Procedures in the Decisional Process, A.B.A. Proc., in 52 F.R.D. 51, 63–65, 68–69, 76–78 (1970)

Johnson, *What Do Law Clerks Do?,* 22 Tex. B.J. 229 (1959)

Judicial Clerkships: A Symposium on the Institution, 26 Vand. L. Rev. 1123 (1973)

Kurland, *Jerome N. Frank, Some Reflections and Recollections of a Law Clerk,* 24 U. Chi. L. Rev. 661 (1957)

Leach, *Recollections of a Holmes Secretary,* 1941 Harv. L. Sch. Bull. 12

Lesinski, *Research Assistants: The Michigan Experience,* 10 Judges' J. 54 (1971).

Llewellyn, *The Common Law Tradition: Deciding Appeals* 321–23 (1960)

McCormack, *A Law Clerk's Recollections,* 46 Colum. L. Rev. 710 (1946).

Meador, *Justice Black and His Law Clerks,* 15 Ala. L. Rev. 57 (1946)

Newland, *Personal Assistants to Supreme Court Justices: The Law Clerks,* 40 Or. L. Rev. 299 (1961)

Oakley & Thompson, Law Clerks and the Judicial Process, Perceptions of the Qualities and Functions of Law Clerks in American Courts (1980)

Sarshik, *The Supreme Court and Its Clerks: Bullets or Blanks for the Hired Guns?*, 1974 Juris Dr. 40

CHAPTER 2. CONDUCT, PROTOCOL, AND ETHICS

§ 1. Conduct
§ 2. Protocol and Ethics

§ 1. Conduct

Those who work in the judicial branch of the government must maintain exceptionally high standards of conduct. Not only judges, but their staffs, officials under their control, and all other employees of the judiciary should strive to maintain public confidence in the federal court system. The following survey of statutes, regulations, and resolutions of the Judicial Conference pertaining to the conduct of judicial employees and officials is not comprehensive, but it points out a few areas of special concern.

CONDUCT EXPECTED OF THE LAW CLERK

The clerk plays an important role in the judicial process and must strive to maintain its integrity. Because of the close association between the judge and the clerk, the clerk's actions, both professional and personal, reflect on the judge and ultimately on the judiciary as a whole. The clerk is therefore held to the very highest standards of conduct. The clerk, like the judge, holds a position of public trust and must comply with the demanding requisites of that position.

CODES OF CONDUCT FOR THIRD BRANCH PERSONNEL

The Judicial Conference of the United States sets administrative policy for the federal courts. In 1973, the Conference adopted a resolution making the 1972 Code of Judicial Conduct of the American Bar Association (drafted originally for state judicial personnel) applicable to federal judges, with a few amendments and exceptions. This code is a successor to the ABA Canons of Judicial Ethics, first adopted in 1924. The Conference has since adopted similar codes of conduct for certain other officers and employees of the federal courts, including law clerks. Appendix B to this handbook contains a portion of the 1973 report of the Judicial Conference adopting, with modifications, the Code of Judicial Conduct; this reprinted portion includes the major statutes and Conference resolutions regarding ethics adopted prior to the adoption of the Code of Judicial Conduct.

CODE OF CONDUCT FOR LAW CLERKS

The Conference adopted the Code of Conduct for Law Clerks in March 1981 and it was last amended in 1988. This code is reprinted as Appendix A to this handbook. The Code's seven canons are generally similar to those in the Code of Judicial Conduct and should be followed in resolving ethical problems. In situations to which the Code is not specifically applicable, it furnishes guidance. Further guidance in interpreting the Code may be sought from the Advisory Committee on the Codes of Conduct, and from various statutes and Judicial Conference resolutions.

ADVISORY COMMITTEE ON THE CODES OF CONDUCT

In 1979, the Conference established its Advisory Committee on Codes of Conduct; persons covered by one of the codes adopted by the Conference may telephone or write the Committee, through its chairman, with questions about the applicability of the particular code to a contemplated action. The Committee's guidance is advisory, however; in the case of a law clerk, the final decision in any ethical situation is that of the clerk, in consultation with the judge for whom the clerk works.

The Advisory Committee should not be confused with another Conference committee, the Judicial Ethics Committee. Creation of the Judicial Ethics Committee was mandated by statute and the Committee was directed to receive financial disclosure reports (generally referred to by the form number, AO-10) from federal judges, magistrates, and judicial employees compensated in excess of the salary for grade 16 of the General Schedule; therefore, law clerks are not required to complete this form.

JUDICIAL CONFERENCE RESOLUTION AGAINST
THE PRACTICE OF LAW

Section D of Canon 5 of the Code of Conduct for Law Clerks forbids law practice by clerks. In addition, a resolution of the Judicial Conference adopted in 1958 states:

> [N]o person employed on a full-time basis in the federal judicial establishment shall engage in the private practice of law. [Judicial Conference Report, September 1958, p. 18.]

The rationale for applying this rule to clerks is clear: first, the practice of law would threaten to raise serious conflicts between a clerk's obligations as a judicial employee, bound to impartiality, and a lawyer's obligation to represent a client fully; second, it would be nearly impossible for a clerk to perform adequately as a clerk, with current heavy caseloads, and still have time for another job.

CONFLICTS OF INTEREST: STATUTORY PROVISIONS

18 U.S.C. § 203 prohibits any officer or employee in the executive, legislative, or judicial branch from asking for or receiving compensation for "services rendered" in relation to any proceeding, determination, ruling, or matter in which the government has an interest. 18 U.S.C. § 205 prohibits government officers or employees from acting on behalf of individuals as attorneys or agents in matters affecting the government; e.g., this section prohibits a law clerk from acting as representative for an individual prosecuting a claim against the United States.

POLITICAL ACTIVITY

Canon 7 of the Code of Conduct for Law Clerks states, "A law clerk should refrain from political activity." A September 1943 Judicial Conference resolution states that judicial branch employees should not participate in the kind of political activity forbidden to executive branch employees by the Hatch Act. The Hatch Act is codified in titles 5 and 18 of the U.S. Code. The general prohibition against influencing elections or taking part in political campaigns found in 5 U.S.C. § 7324 was upheld in U.S. Civil Service

Commission v. Letter Carriers, 413 U.S. 548 (1973). Thus, while the Hatch Act does not directly apply to law clerks, its proscriptions and interpretations should be considered mandatory with respect to their conduct.

A clerk may of course entertain personal views on political questions and is not required to surrender the prerogatives of citizenship, but the clerkship must be, at the least, a sabbatical from active political involvement.

The clerk should never, even in private conversation, quote the judge's political views or attribute to the judge any position on any political issue. When asked about the judge's opinion concerning any such matter, clerks must indicate that they are not in a position to express it or to comment on it. The clerk must also abstain from any discussion, formal or informal, of the judge's position on any particular legal or social issue. If judges wish to publish their thoughts about jurisprudential, economic, or social issues, they know how to do so.

NEPOTISM AND FAVORITISM

The Code of Judicial Conduct, Canon 3 B(4), states:

> A judge should not make unnecessary appointments. A judge should exercise the power of appointment *only on the basis of merit, avoiding nepotism and favoritism.* (Emphasis supplied.)

The U.S. Code also prohibits nepotism or favoritism in employment. 28 U.S.C. § 458 provides:

> No person shall be appointed to or employed in any office or duty in any court who is related by affinity or consanguinity within the degree of first cousin to any justice or judge of such court.

Another provision, 5 U.S.C. § 3110(b), in part provides:

> A public official may not appoint, employ, promote, advance, or advocate for appointment, employment, or advancement, in or to a civilian position in the agency in which he is serving or over which he exercises jurisdiction or control any individual who is a relative of the public official. [The term "relative" is defined in 5 U.S.C. 3110(a)(3).]

The penalty for violation of these provisions is denial of pay to the appointee. These laws are applicable to all appointments within the judicial branch, whether made by a judge, U.S. magistrate, clerk of the court, probation officer, or similar person. Moreover, the Judicial Conference of the United States at its October 1940 meeting resolved:

> No person should hereafter be appointed as law clerk or secretary to a circuit or district judge who is related to the judge concerned within the degree of affinity or consanguinity described in [28 U.S.C. § 458].

Although judges interpret these precepts differently, most consider themselves prohibited both from hiring relatives or the children of close friends and from prevailing on other judges in the same court to do so. Though these rules may result in denial of a clerkship position to an otherwise qualified applicant, they do prevent criticism, no matter how unfounded, of the court as an institution run for the personal benefit of a judge and the judge's family and friends. Inquiries regarding the propriety of hiring a particular individual may be referred to the General Counsel's Office of the Administrative Office.

§ 2. Protocol and Ethics

THE JUDGE AND THE LAW CLERK

The relationship between the judge and the law clerk has several facets: employer–employee, teacher–student, and lawyer–lawyer. In all of these the clerk must be aware of the respect due to the judge. Respect does not mean subservience: A clerk should not fear to express an opinion contrary to the judge's when asked, and most judges expect and invite their clerks to question the judge's views. Judges frequently seek the reactions of their clerks to the issues raised in pending cases, both for the value of being exposed to varying viewpoints and to train their clerks in the process of legal decision-making. Judges may also ask clerks to express an independent view after reaching a tentative decision. They may do this to test the clerk's conclusion or reasoning abilities. Clerks should, therefore, present their views when asked. If, however, the judge should then reach a conclusion that differs from the clerk's, the clerk should carry out the judge's instructions with the utmost fidelity. The ultimate responsibility for fulfilling the duties of the judge's office is the judge's. One judge put it pithily: "The commission from the President issues to me, not my law clerk, and it was I who took the oath of office."

LOYALTY

The clerk owes the judge complete confidentiality, accuracy, and loyalty. The judge relies upon the clerk's research in reaching conclusions on pending cases. The judge relies on confidentiality in discussing performance of judicial duties, and the judge must be able to count on complete loyalty. The clerk must not criticize the judge's decisions or work habits to anyone, even other members of the same court. As Judge Ruggero J. Aldisert put it:

> A judge's law clerk is a confidant. More than any other experience in preparing for a career in the legal profession, a clerkship is grounded on notions of confidentiality, pervasive in the practice of law. The judge–clerk relationship is as sacred as that of priest–penitent. Indeed, to emphasize the importance of this relationship, I give new law clerks a formal message:

> I have retained you as researchers and editors, but you are also my lawyers. As lawyers, you are absolutely forbidden to disclose the intimate details of this lawyer–client relationship, of the decisionmaking and decision-justifying processes that take place in these chambers. This court is a family, and there will be times that I will make remarks about my family members. They will be uttered sometimes in the heat of passion or despair. They will not be repeated beyond the chambers door. Even if I occasionally blow off steam, remember that these judges are my colleagues and will be my friends long after you are gone from here.

Aldisert, Review of Schwartz, *Super Chief: Earl Warren and His Supreme Court,* 72 Calif. L. Rev. 275, 282 (1984).

A clerk should never comment on the judge's views or work habits, or offer a personal appraisal of the judge's opinions. Even when directly asked, the clerk should say only something like, "I enjoy working for the judge and I cannot comment beyond that." The judge is the only person who can or should communicate to the bar whatever personal data the judge wishes to be generally known.

THE PUBLIC AND THE LAW CLERK

The courts are a public-service organization and the public properly expects efficient service of professional quality. The public generally is unfamiliar with the court system, and its opportunities to view the system in operation are infrequent. Every effort should be made to assist the public, including witnesses or jurors. The brief encounter that jurors or witnesses have with the federal court system may greatly influence their evaluation of the quality and efficiency of that system.

Courtesy and kindness must not include advice. The clerk must not answer questions about the case from witnesses or jurors. The clerk should report to the judge any question or inquiry by a witness or juror that relates to the case.

AVOIDANCE OF PUBLIC STATEMENT BY A LAW CLERK REGARDING PENDING OR PAST PROCEEDINGS

The law clerk's position requires discretion. The clerk must avoid any hint about the judge's likely action in a case. After the judge acts, the action and, if there is an opinion, the reasoning underlying the action are matters of public record. The law clerk should not comment on them or try to explain them. The clerk must scrupulously resist the temptation to discuss interesting pending or decided cases among friends or family. Even discussions with clerks from other chambers should be circumspect. Indeed, some judges forbid their clerks to discuss any pending cases even with other clerks.

Many district courts have rules forbidding court personnel to divulge information about pending cases. If friends, representatives of news media, or others inquire concerning any proceeding, the clerk should refer them to the official record in the office of the clerk of court.

THE ATTORNEYS AND THE LAW CLERK

The clerk should be friendly, courteous, and helpful to lawyers. At the same time, the clerk must be firm in resisting any effort to gain improper advantage, to win favor, or to enlist sympathy.

A law clerk may not reveal to an attorney anything that the clerk could not reveal to the public generally. The clerk should not engage in any informal discussion with an attorney about a pending case or a decision that has been reached by the judge. Whatever the attorney has to say about a case should be set forth in a written pleading, memorandum, or letter or by oral argument. Almost despite themselves, some few lawyers, perhaps because of their instincts as advocates, may attempt to gain information from a law clerk ex parte or to make an ex parte plea about the equity or justice of the result the lawyer is seeking. The clerk must terminate any efforts to do this, politely but firmly, as soon as the conversation begins and refer the attorney to the judge. The clerk should not allow any lawyer to communicate any kind of ex parte information regarding the merit or lack of merit of a particular case. Opposing counsel should always have notice and fair opportunity to respond to any presentation made by an attorney to the court. Ex parte communications create the atmosphere of partiality and potential unfairness, and are of questionable value because the opposition may have a valid contrary argument that goes unheard.

Some judges forbid their clerks to have any communication with lawyers. The clerk for a judge who has this rule must respect it scrupulously.

Many other judges expect their clerks to communicate or deal with lawyers in respect to some matters, such as scheduling. These judges want their clerks to· be helpful and cooperative, but nevertheless to avoid doing anything that will compromise the judge or the court staff. The clerks for judges who have this policy should follow these precepts:

1. The clerk should not give any advice on matters of substantive law.

2. If the lawyer asks about either local procedure or general federal procedure for handling a matter, the clerk may read to the lawyer, or refer the lawyer to, either the appro-

priate federal rule or local court rule. If the question relates to the judge's personal practice with respect to handling matters (for example, how the judge handles requests for temporary restraining orders), the clerk may tell the lawyer what the clerk knows. The clerk should not guess at what the judge does or may do. If not certain about the judge's policy, the clerk should say something like, "I don't know what the judge would like a lawyer to do in these circumstances, but I'll be glad to consult the judge about the problem and call you back."

3. The clerk should not allow a lawyer to coax the clerk into doing research, even the most minor.

4. The clerk should not hesitate to issue a disclaimer on any information the clerk may give. Almost all attorneys understand such a position. ("I can't give you any legal advice, as you understand. However, you may find it helpful to look at local rule 3.09.")

5. When in doubt, the clerk should politely decline to give information. ("I'm really sorry I can't help you, but Judge X has instructed me not to answer that kind of question.")

Those judges who wish their law clerks to communicate with counsel about scheduling or other matters do not wish the conversation to stray into anything that might reflect the judge's (or the law clerk's) attitude about the issues in the case or their merits. The sole authority on substantive or procedural issues is the judge, who communicates with the attorneys either verbally or through written opinions. Any expression by the clerk to an attorney about a pending case may either raise the expectations or dash the hopes of the lawyer—in either situation without authority or propriety. Such expressions impute exaggerated importance to the clerk and destroy faith in the deliberative nature of the judicial process.

NEUTRALITY AND IMPARTIALITY

All attorneys should be given impartial and equal treatment. The clerk may be tempted to do a special favor for a law school classmate or an old friend, but the judge and all members of the judge's staff must remain absolutely neutral toward all parties and attorneys involved.

Problems may be created if a clerk is applying for a position with a lawyer or law firm then appearing in pending cases. That problem is discussed in the section entitled "Restrictions on Involvement of Law Clerks in Cases of Attorneys with Whom Applications for Employment Are Pending," at p. 23.

COURTROOM DEMEANOR: TRIALS

The clerk, like the judge, is required to be impartial. During a jury trial, physical cues within view of the jurors reduce that impartiality and may unfairly influence the jury. A clerk must avoid body or facial movements or expressions that might indicate to the jury the clerk's reaction to testimony of witnesses or to oral arguments of attorneys, even during a bench trial or appellate argument, because impartiality and objectivity should be maintained in all cases not only by those who serve as impartial arbiters of justice but also by all others who are officially attached to the court. Indeed, litigants are more likely to expect and understand reflections of attitude by the judge, who has a duty to control proceedings and to decide the case, than by the judge's assistants.

DRESS

Most judges do not have a dress code but do expect professional dress and behavior, the kind that would be appropriate in a professional office.

INFORMING THE JUDGE OF INFORMATION
RECEIVED INFORMALLY

The judge should be apprised of informal communications to clerks regarding pending cases. For example, an attorney may call to state that there is no objection to a pending motion, or that both attorneys jointly request the continuance of a hearing. Because of the impact of these events on docket management or their effect on the trial calendar, the judge may wish to take some action. For example, the judge may wish to call a conference of counsel, or to devote increased attention to another matter for which immediate preparation is necessary. Informal information can save the judge and the staff wasted effort.

A dilemma arises when the clerk receives specific information about the progress of settlement negotiations in a case in which the judge is to be the trier of fact. Ordinarily, settlement proposals or discussions are inadmissible, and therefore some judges shield themselves from knowledge of specific settlement proposals that might affect their judgment. Other judges either like to, or are willing to, have such information because they believe that they can nonetheless judge the facts fairly and remain uninfluenced by settlement proposals. A clerk must be guided by the individual policy of the judge in this regard.

THE MEDIA AND THE LAW CLERK

Journalists frequently telephone chambers to inquire about a case, or attempt to provoke a conversation at a social affair. There should be as little communication as possible between the clerk and representatives of the media. The clerk should determine the policy of the judge and answer inquiries from members of the media accordingly. Some judges refer all questions to the clerk of court. Other judges direct the clerk of court to distribute opinions or judgments that have already been made public and filed of record by the judge.

PRIOR NOTICE TO COUNSEL

In cases of interest to the general public or to the media, some judges may wish to notify the attorneys in the case in advance when a prospective judgment, opinion, or order is to be filed, except when such information might provide the attorneys and parties with "inside" information of potentially significant economic advantage. Such notice enables counsel to read the opinion at the moment it is filed and notify their clients of the result. Attorneys appreciate the opportunity of being the first to notify their clients, and clients themselves may wish to notify other interested parties of the result. Some embarrassment and confusion may result if the parties to a suit first hear of a ruling through the media. Moreover, media reports are often incomplete and may create misimpressions of the actual nature of a ruling. Unless the judge instructs the clerk otherwise, however, if an attorney asks when an opinion will be rendered, the clerk should always indicate that such information is confidential.

RULES REGARDING THE MEDIA IN COURT

The Judicial Conference of the United States in 1979 adopted the following resolution, based on Rule 53 of the Federal Rules of Criminal Procedure:

> RESOLVED, That the Judicial Conference of the United States condemns the taking of photographs in the courtroom or its environs in connection with any judicial proceedings, and the broadcasting of judicial proceedings by radio, television, or other means, and considers such practices to be inconsistent with fair judicial procedure and that they ought not to be permitted in any federal court. A judge may, however, permit broadcasting, televising, recording or photographing of investitive, ceremonial, or naturalization proceedings.

In September 1984 the Conference denied a petition filed by various news media groups requesting that Canon 3(A)(7) of the Code of Judicial Conduct, Rule 53 of the Federal Rules of Criminal Procedure, and the Federal Rules of Appellate Procedure be amended to allow broadcast and still camera coverage of federal court proceedings.

Code of Judicial Conduct Canon 3(A)(7) recognizes the exception for the taking of photographs at certain ceremonial and other court proceedings. That canon states:

> (7) A judge should prohibit broadcasting, televising, recording, or taking photographs in courtrooms and areas immediately adjacent thereto during sessions of court, or recesses between sessions, except that under rules prescribed by a supervising appellate court or other appropriate authority, a judge may authorize broadcasting, televising, recording and photographing of judicial proceedings in courtrooms and areas immediately adjacent thereto consistent with the right of the parties to a fair trial and subject to express conditions, limitations, and guidelines which allow such coverage in a manner that will be unobtrusive, will not distract the trial participants, and will not otherwise interfere with the administration of justice.

In addition, many district and appellate courts have adopted local rules with specific instructions regarding photographing of court proceedings and other relationships of the media to the judicial system. Every clerk should review and be familiar with any local rule of the district or circuit relating to this topic, and should assist in the enforcement of that rule.

Although local rules restrict the *means* by which news may be reported (e.g., no cameras or broadcasting from the courtroom or environs), "there is nothing that proscribes the press from reporting events that transpire in the courtroom." Sheppard v. Maxwell, 384 U.S. 333, 362–63 (1966). *See also* Nebraska Press Ass'n v. Stuart, 427 U.S. 539 (1976). The Constitution creates a presumption that trials will be open. Press-Enterprise Co. v. Superior Court, 464 U.S. 501 (1984). This does not necessarily apply to pretrial proceedings, Waller v. Georgia, 467 U.S. 39 (1984), but it does apply to argument of cases in both trial and appellate courts.

RESTRICTIONS ON INVOLVEMENT OF LAW CLERKS IN CASES OF ATTORNEYS WITH WHOM APPLICATIONS FOR EMPLOYMENT ARE PENDING

Application by a clerk to a firm that has cases pending before the judge may create problems for the law firm, the judge, and the clerk. Practices regarding this matter vary. Some judges instruct their clerks not to apply for jobs and not to have interviews with law firms until near the end of the clerkship. Others permit applications, but build a "Chinese Wall" around the clerk concerning matters in which that firm is involved, requiring another clerk to handle such matters. The clerk should learn the judge's policy and follow it. In any event, even if no restrictions are placed on a clerk's applications for employment while clerking, a common-sense rule is that a clerk should carefully avoid even the most indirect discussion of cases pending before the judge during interviews and all other communications with the firm.

When a clerk has accepted a position with an attorney or with a firm, that clerk should cease further involvement in those cases in which the future employer has an interest. With the judge's permission, the clerk should transfer those cases to another clerk and receive others in exchange.

RESTRICTIONS ON LAW PRACTICE AFTER TERMINATION OF A
CLERKSHIP: CASES IN WHICH THE LAW CLERK WAS INVOLVED
AND APPEARING BEFORE THE JUDGE FOR WHOM
THE LAW CLERK WORKED

Many courts or individual judges place restrictions on a law clerk's professional activities after the end of the clerkship. These may include: (a) prohibitions from ever participating in any form in any case pending during the clerkship and (b) prohibitions from appearing as an attorney in the court in which the clerk served, usually for one or two years. The clerk must determine the policy of both the court and the judge. In any event, former clerks must not participate in any way in any case in which they performed any work of any kind while clerks. The ABA's Model Rules of Professional Responsibility also prohibit lawyers from representing a client in a case on which the lawyer worked previously as a public officer or employee. Some courts have adopted rules relating to these matters and the clerk is of course bound to follow these rules.

CHAPTER 3. BASIC ANALYSIS OF LITIGATION CONDUCTED IN U.S. COURTS

The conduct of litigation in the federal courts is governed by a number of uniformly applicable rules: the Federal Rules of Civil Procedure, the Federal Rules of Criminal Procedure, the Federal Rules of Appellate Procedure, the Bankruptcy Rules, the Federal Rules of Evidence, and the Trial of Misdemeanor Rules. Those rules are supplemented by the local rules of each individual court. Each law clerk should keep a copy of each of these publications at hand. The following section outlines the steps in the process of civil litigation.

§ 1. The Civil Action

PROCESSING LITIGATION

The major steps in civil cases are listed below.

1. Plaintiff commences action by filing a complaint with the clerk of court;

2. Jurisdiction is obtained over defendant, e.g., by service of process;

3. Defendant files motions, e.g., motion to dismiss for failure to state a claim for which relief may be granted (motions of this type and others may, however, be filed later);

4. Defendant files an answer, which may contain a motion to dismiss;

5. Discovery proceeds;

6. Either party may file additional motions, e.g., summary judgment;

7. Pretrial conference is held;

8. Trial is held;

9. Judgment is rendered, signed, and filed;

10 Post-trial proceedings may occur;

11. Appeal is taken. Judgment may or may not be stayed;

12. Appeal is considered either on briefs or after oral argument;

13. Judgment is rendered on appeal;

14. Supplementary proceedings may occur;

15. Judgment is enforced.

In any given case some of these steps may be omitted as a result of inaction, agreement of the parties, or court order. And, of course, the suit may end by settlement or judgment of dismissal at any stage. Fewer than 10 percent of all civil actions continue to trial, but the court will have to decide motions in nearly all civil cases. In some cases the motions alone may ultimately fill several case files.

COMMENCEMENT OF ACTION

A civil action in a federal court begins with the filing of a written complaint in the clerk's office. The case is then assigned a number, usually referred to as a "docket number." The docket number contains two parts: The first part contains the last two digits of the year in which the case was filed; the second part is a number that is assigned consecutively as suits are filed in each calendar year, beginning with number 101. The prefix, Cr. or C.A., indicates whether the case is a criminal or civil action. As an example, the thirty-seventh civil case filed in 1988 would be assigned the number C.A. 88-137. In a multi-judge court, the clerk's office through a preestablished random selection process immediately assigns the case to a particular judge for handling and ultimate disposition. The clerk then adds a section designation, usually a letter, to the docket number to indicate the section of the district court to which the case has been assigned or to indicate in which division of the court the case was filed.

The clerk's office maintains (a) the complete record of the case, (b) a case file, or docket sheet, which includes notations to reflect the progress of the case, and (c) alphabetical indices by parties' names, which allow retrieval of the number of a case. Each month the clerk's office submits a statistical report to the Administrative Office describing each case that has been filed (Form J.S. 5).

In most cases there is little to be done in the judge's office when the case is filed except to make such record entries as may be used by the judge to monitor and control the progress of cases assigned. If, however, there is a request for a temporary restraining order or other immediate emergency relief or the case is a class action, early attention to the case is required.

The local rules of court usually require the lawyer who files a class action to indicate its nature by a caption on the first page of the complaint. Fed. R. Civ. P. 23(c)(1) requires: "As soon as practicable after the commencement of an action brought as a class action, the court shall determine by order whether it is to be so maintained." The judge will usually wish, therefore, to be alerted to the filing of this kind of case promptly. Other proceedings requiring prompt action by the court are discussed separately below.

MULTIDISTRICT LITIGATION PROBLEMS

The functions of the Judicial Panel on Multidistrict Litigation are discussed at p. 76. Generally if civil actions involving one or more common questions of fact are pending in different districts either plaintiff or defendant will petition the panel to transfer the cases to a single district and to consolidate them for pretrial proceedings. The rules of the panel may be found at the statutory section on multidistrict litigation, 28 U.S.C. § 1407, and in the *Manual for Complex Litigation, Second,* available in the judge's library. If the panel decides that the cases should be consolidated, it enters an appropriate order and all of the cases are then transferred to the district designated by the panel.

The district judge may invoke intervention of the panel by writing the Judicial Panel on Multidistrict Litigation at the address in the *United States Court Directory.* The letter will say that the court has a case that may be related to another case or cases pending in another district, giving the name and docket number of each case, and that it might be worthwhile for the panel to examine these cases to determine whether consolidation would be appropriate. The judge will attach to the letter a copy of the complaint in the case pending in the judge's court and any other documents that may be useful to the panel.

Any questions about multidistrict litigation procedures should be directed to the clerk of the panel, who is listed in the *United States Court Directory*.

OBTAINING JURISDICTION OVER THE DEFENDANT

After the complaint is filed, the clerk of court (through a deputy clerk) issues a summons to each defendant named in the complaint directing that defendant to serve an answer to the complaint on counsel for the plaintiff and advising that, if the defendant fails to do so, a default judgment will be entered. The summons is signed by the clerk and bears the court seal.

The clerk delivers the summons to the plaintiff or the plaintiff's lawyer, who is responsible for prompt service of the summons together with a copy of the complaint. Service of process may be accomplished in the manner permitted by the law of the state in which the district court is held or by mail, as prescribed by Fed. R. Civ. P. 4(c)(2)(C). Service is made by a marshal only:

(1)   on behalf of a party proceeding in forma pauperis;

(2)   on behalf of the United States or an officer or agency of the United States; or

(3)   pursuant to a court order stating that a U.S. marshal or deputy marshal, or another person specially appointed for the purpose of serving process, is required to serve the summons and complaint in order that service can be properly effected in that particular action.

The person who makes service is required to execute a return showing that service has been made. Fed. R. Civ. P. 4(g).

If service is not made within 120 days after filing the complaint, and the party on whose behalf service was required cannot show good cause why service has not been made within that period, the action must be dismissed as to any defendant not served, without prejudice, upon the court's own initiative after notice to the party who failed to make service or upon motion. Fed. R. Civ. P. 4(j).

MOTION PRACTICE

After the complaint is filed, the defendant may respond with motions, an answer, or both. A clerk may be asked to perform any or all of the following duties in connection with a motion:

1. Maintain in-office records and call to the judge's attention motions that are ready for decision;

2. Read and analyze the motion and any responses and briefs;

3. Perform independent research supplementary to that contained in the briefs of the parties;

4. Attend evidentiary hearings and oral arguments;

5. Prepare memoranda for use by the judge regarding factual or legal issues presented by the motion;

6. Discuss the motion with the judge; and

7. Draft for the approval of the judge an order disposing of the motion.

The motions most frequently filed early in the proceedings are those challenging the jurisdiction of the court over the parties or the subject matter, attacking venue, raising issues relating to joinder of parties, and denying the legal sufficiency of the complaint. Because, under Fed. R. Civ. P. 12(a), these motions suspend the time for answering the complaint, a motion that has no real merit may be presented for dilatory reasons. To deal with this possibility many courts have adopted local rules requiring the moving party to file a separate brief in support of the motion; if counsel fails to do so, the motion is treated as abandoned. Some courts refuse to accept a motion for filing with the clerk unless a memorandum of law is filed simultaneously. Although some courts do not require reply memoranda, opposing counsel is usually required to file a memorandum of law if the motion is opposed.

Upon receipt of a motion or a response to a motion, the clerk of court makes appropriate record entries and then routes the motion and supporting papers to the judge assigned to the case. Many courts require all motions, responses to motions, and supporting memoranda to be filed in duplicate so that one copy may be retained in the record and the other used in the judge's chambers. The judge's office usually maintains a list of all pending motions.

Some judges hear oral argument on all motions. Others hear oral argument on a motion only if the judge schedules argument. Those judges require moving counsel to request oral argument in the body of the motion, state the reason why counsel believes oral argument would be helpful to the court, and provide an estimate of the time required for the argument. The court may then, in its discretion, set the motion for argument and notify counsel in writing of the day and time. Still other courts hear argument unless the judge has notified counsel that the matter will be decided on the briefs. The practice of the judge for whom the clerk is working is of course controlling.

The local rules of the district court usually require a moving party who wishes a hearing on the motion to give notice when the motion will be heard a certain number of days in advance of the scheduled hearing date. They also usually require opposing counsel to respond at least a certain number of days after the motion is filed or a certain number of days before the date set for hearing.

Some motions involve disputed factual issues and therefore require evidentiary hearings. These, and all motions for which the judge has requested oral argument, must be scheduled at times convenient to the court and, insofar as possible, to counsel and witnesses. Four different approaches to scheduling have been adopted:

1. Selection of a specific date and time by the judge or judge's staff with notice to both counsel;

2. Selection of a date and time convenient to all involved after telephone or personal conferences among counsel and court personnel;

3. Selection of a date and time acceptable to the court by one attorney who then gives notice to other counsel; and

4. Permanent scheduling by the court of a weekly or monthly "motion day" at which any motions that are at issue may be heard as a matter of course, or, alternatively, for which particular motions are scheduled through one of the first three described processes.

In some courts in which a number of motions are heard on a single day, the following procedure is used. Several days in advance, the docket clerk or courtroom deputy prepares a list of the motions to be heard on a particular day, including the name of the case and docket number. A law clerk then assembles for each motion the record, a copy of each memorandum, and all other relevant materials. These are brought to the courtroom a short time before the opening of court and are placed close to the judge's bench. A large number of motions may be scheduled, and the assembly of records and materials may be time-consuming; organization and preparation are the keys to efficiency. Attorneys in a case are responsible for ensuring that witnesses are present at evidentiary hearings voluntarily or through use of subpoena. To avoid protracted waiting periods for other lawyers who have motions to be heard on the same day, most courts that have a regular "motion day" do not permit testimony to be heard on that day without a special order from the judge.

In those courts that hear oral argument on a number of motions on the same day, it is not unusual for the court to receive requests for the continuance of the argument on motions. The motion may have been set originally by one lawyer without finding out whether opposing counsel had a prior commitment on that day; lawyers may have oral arguments scheduled before more than one judge on the same day; opposing counsel may request more time to study the law and facts and to prepare a memorandum opposing the motion; or the lawyers may believe they can resolve the issue between themselves. For any of these reasons, one or both lawyers may request a continuance.

Many judges will agree to continue a motion based on a telephone request of a lawyer if the lawyer advises the judge that opposing counsel has been informed of the request and has no objection. Other judges require counsel to file a written motion for a continuance, even when there is no objection by opposing counsel. The motion or an attached memorandum must state the reason for the continuance and fix a day on which the motion will be heard.

The clerk usually attends the motions-day arguments to assist the judge by making available the materials relevant to a particular motion, by noting any new authority cited by either counsel, and, if the judge decides the motion from the bench, by making notes of the judge's decision on a particular motion (though the courtroom deputy officially records the court's judgment or decision and the judge later signs a summary order prepared by that deputy or submitted by prevailing counsel).

When all responses and briefs have been filed or the allowed time has elapsed and, in appropriate cases, oral argument or an evidentiary hearing has been held, the motion is ripe for decision. (The term frequently used is that the motion "is at issue.")

OPINIONS ON MOTIONS UNDER SUBMISSION

Whenever the judge hears argument on a motion and does not rule from the bench, it is necessary to prepare an order disposing of the motion. If the judge instructs the clerk to do this, the clerk should start by asking the judge's secretary for samples of orders previously rendered that can serve as a guide. The judge may instead direct one of the parties to prepare the order for court approval. See discussion on p. 148.

After an order ruling on the motion has been signed, the order is sent to the office of the clerk of court, where appropriate record entries are made. The clerk's office then notifies all attorneys of record of the ruling by the court and the clerk usually sends them a photocopy of the order itself.

Matters taken under submission must be carefully followed to be sure they are decided as promptly as possible. The clerk should keep a list of matters under submission, deleting cases as the ruling on each is completed.

TEMPORARY RESTRAINING ORDERS

The procedural rules governing applications for temporary restraining orders are set forth in Fed. R. Civ. P. 65. When such orders are sought, plaintiff's counsel may assert that the matter is of such urgency as to require an ex parte restraining order, that is, without prior notice to or opportunity to be heard by the defendant. If the judge is not in chambers at that time, the plaintiff's counsel may exhort the clerk to bring the order to the judge in open court, or to locate the judge, or to assist in some other way. The clerk should inquire about the judge's policy on such emergency inquiries so as to be prepared to handle them.

Most district judges will not sign requests for ex parte temporary restraining orders except in rare instances when the matter is of such dire emergency that the exigencies of the situation do not permit the opposing party to be heard, and then only after full compliance with Rule 65(b). If a lawyer comes to the chambers asking to see the judge about signing an ex parte temporary restraining order, some judges may wish their clerks to do the following:

1. Advise the lawyer that the judge does not ordinarily sign temporary restraining orders without hearing what the lawyer for the other side has to say. This may be done by arranging for the judge to see both counsel in person or by a telephone conference, depending on the judge's policy. The clerk should communicate with the judge to determine when the conference should be scheduled.

2. While the lawyer is attempting to arrange the conference, attempt to read all documents pertinent to the request, collect and examine the authorities, and be prepared to brief the judge about the request or to take such other action as the judge may wish.

3. Communicate with the courtroom deputy and the court reporter to arrange for their presence at the conference unless the judge does not require them.

THE ANSWER

Twenty days after the complaint is served or 10 days after notice of disposition of a preliminary motion, the defendant must answer the complaint. If the defendant fails to do so, the plaintiff may have the defendant's default made a matter of record in the clerk's office and then proceed to obtain a default judgment in the manner provided in Fed. R. Civ. P. 55.

In addition to answering the complaint, the defendant may assert a counterclaim against the plaintiff or a cross-claim against another defendant. The person against whom a counterclaim or cross-claim is made has 20 days after service or 10 days after disposition of a motion relating to the counterclaim or cross-claim in which to reply. In the event of a failure to answer, the defendant may obtain a default judgment in accordance with Rule 55.

Many courts permit counsel, by agreement, to extend the time for answering. Other courts believe that an appearance of some kind—even if only to obtain an extension of time—should be made by counsel so that the court can be promptly informed of counsel's identity, and will have the means to determine what progress is being made. To this end, these courts have adopted a rule that provides:

> Upon certification by a moving party that there has been no previous extension of time to plead and that the opposing party has not filed in the record an objection to an extension of time, then on an ex parte motion and order, the court will allow one extension for a period of 20 days from the time the pleading would otherwise be due. Further extensions will not be granted by stipulation but only after motion noticed for hearing according to the regular motion procedure.

Motions relating to third-party practice or relating to jurisdiction over or sufficiency of a counterclaim or cross-claim may be filed at this stage of the proceedings. They are processed in the same manner as preliminary motions.

THE DORMANT ACTION

Most federal courts do not permit actions to remain dormant for an indefinite period of time. Each court, and sometimes the judges within each court, will have a different policy with respect to this. Counsel have their own priorities for processing litigation, and these frequently relate to their own internal office demands and other personal matters. In general, however, the policy of the federal courts is that litigation is not merely the lawyers' business but is also the public's business and that the court has responsibility for monitoring litigation once it is filed in court.

To fulfill this responsibility, many courts have the docket clerk or someone in the clerk of court's office periodically call to the judge's attention cases that have been dormant for more than six months, or some other period of time, either because no answer has been filed or because, after pleadings were filed, no further action has been taken. Many judges will have a periodic "call docket," at which counsel will be asked to report on the status of cases that have been dormant for a period of time and explain why no progress has been made in the case. In some instances, failure of counsel to appear at the call docket results in dismissal of the case.

MOTION PRACTICE AFTER ANSWER

Discovery Motions and Schedules

The purpose of discovery is to allow each party to obtain relevant evidence or sources of relevant evidence from other parties and to avoid evidentiary surprise at the time of trial. General provisions governing discovery are set forth in Fed. R. Civ. P. 20. The specific discovery methods available to a party are:

1. Deposition upon oral examination (Rule 30);

2. Deposition upon written questions (Rule 31);

3. Written interrogatories (Rule 33);

4. Production of documents or things (Rule 34);

5. Permission to enter upon land or other property for inspection and other purposes (Rule 34);

6. Physical and mental examinations (Rule 35); and

7. Requests for admissions of fact (Rule 36).

In routine cases counsel conduct discovery proceedings without direct initial court involvement. Fed. R. Civ. P. 16, however, permits the judge to intervene at an early stage in the suit to assume judicial control over its progress and schedule dates for completion of the principal pretrial steps, including discovery. The rule mandates a pretrial scheduling order except in categories of actions exempted by local rule as inappropriate. In complex cases, in cases assigned by the Judicial Panel on Multidistrict Litigation, and in cases in which the court is attempting to reduce the time spent in discovery, the court also becomes directly involved by scheduling times and places for discovery activities and otherwise monitoring and supervising such proceedings.

A variety of motions may arise as a result of discovery proceedings, including those:

1. To compel answers or other compliance with discovery rules;

2. To obtain protective orders against undue harassment, unreasonable demands, or disclosure of confidential or protected information;

3. To obtain additional time to comply with discovery requests;

4. To pose objections to written interrogatories or other discovery requests; and

5. To impose sanctions for failure to comply with discovery requests.

Fed. R. Civ. P. 26 prescribes general rules governing discovery. In many courts, all motions pertaining to discovery are referred to a magistrate, as is responsibility for overseeing discovery procedures and ruling on discovery motions. The magistrate's orders may be appealed to the district judge.

Summary Judgment Motions

During discovery or after its completion, other motions may be filed. These tend to fall into two categories:

1. Motions for summary judgment as to some or all of the issues raised in the case (Rule 56); and

2. Motions to amend pleadings or to add or remove parties (Rule 15).

Both usually arise out of information obtained by the moving party during discovery. They are processed in the same manner as other motions.

PRETRIAL CONFERENCE

The pretrial conference is governed by Fed. R. Civ. P. 16 and is intended to simplify the subsequent trial. Whether a conference is held in a specific case is discretionary with the court, and the practice varies substantially throughout the federal judiciary. In some courts a pretrial conference is routinely held in each case, while in others a conference is held only when requested by counsel or ordered by the court.

Typically the conference is held only after discovery has been completed (or when nearly complete) at a time when counsel are fully aware of the evidence in the case. In complex cases, however, a pretrial conference may be held early in the proceedings to establish discovery schedules and other preliminary matters. Additional conferences may be conducted as the case progresses.

Before a pretrial conference the clerk should review the case file, put the documents in sequence, and place both the file and the record at the place designated by the judge in the judge's chambers. This should be done sufficiently in advance of the conference to allow the judge time to look through the file. If a proposed pretrial order has been submitted, the order should be placed at the top of the file.

Some judges wish the courtroom deputy or the clerk or both to attend pretrial conferences. Others permit their clerks to attend selected conferences of interest. During the first month or two after beginning work, the clerk should attend as often as possible to gain insight into the conference procedure.

During the conference the judge and counsel may consider any "matters that may aid in the disposition of the action." The matters most commonly considered are:

1. Simplification of the issues;

2. Necessary or desirable amendments to the pleadings;

3. The avoidance of unnecessary evidence at trial by obtaining admissions of uncontested facts;

4. Limitation of the number of expert witnesses;

5. Referral of issues to a special master;

6. Exchange of lists of witnesses;

7. Marking of exhibits;

8. Final discovery procedures; and

9. Discussion of settlement.

In many courts counsel are required to file and exchange detailed pretrial memoranda containing information relating to the matters to be considered at the conference.

The conference itself may be held in chambers, with or without a court reporter, or may be conducted as a formal hearing in open court.

Some courts have adopted a local rule prescribing the pretrial procedure. In other courts, judges may issue mimeographed or photocopied descriptions of their pretrial procedure. The clerk should inquire about the judge's practice, study any applicable court rule or standing order, and be prepared to assist in any way possible.

PRETRIAL ORDERS

In civil cases other than those involving simple issues of law or fact, Fed. R. Civ. P. 16 requires a scheduling order and specifies matters to be discussed at any pretrial conference held pursuant to the rule, followed by a pretrial order. Almost all district courts have adopted a form for the pretrial order. Usually the court requires the pretrial order to contain a concise summary of disputed issues of fact and disputed issues of law, a succinct statement of the position of each party, and a list of the witnesses and documents expected to be introduced at trial. In some districts, the final pretrial order must be presented to the court at least 24 hours before the face-to-face pretrial conference, which is held with all lawyers and the judge attending. Other courts require only that counsel bring the pretrial order with them to the conference.

Preparation of a detailed pretrial order often requires a substantial amount of time. Judges differ on whether the results warrant the effort. Those judges who require such an order usually demand that the opposing attorneys meet face to face to prepare it, and its preparation requires counsel to be familiar with the case both from their point of view and their opponents'. Most judges think that a properly prepared pretrial order makes for a more efficient trial. Most judges consider a pretrial order essential to conducting an orderly and efficient trial of a complicated case. In simpler cases, judges may require counsel to prepare only a list of witnesses and exhibits.

After the pretrial order is signed by the judge and the lawyers at the pretrial conference, most judges will not allow amendments to include new witnesses or documents unless special justification is shown for their not having been included originally.

The clerk should learn not only what the local rules of court require with respect to pretrial orders and conferences but also the practice of the judge for whom the clerk is working, for an individual judge may wish the lawyers to incorporate something more or less than the local rules require.

SANCTIONS

At least since the 1970s, many judges and lawyers have been concerned about abuse of the litigative process—for example, about attorneys who file needless motions or are unprepared for trial or pretrial events. In 1983, the Judicial Conference proposed and the Congress accepted amendments to the Federal Rules of Civil Procedure to deal with this perceived problem. These amendments—to Rules 7, 11, and 16—direct or authorize the judge to impose sanctions on attorneys or parties or both if, for example, motions are not filed in good faith or attorneys are unprepared to participate in pretrial conferences. Judges differ in their propensity to impose sanctions and in their view of the proper severity of sanctions. The clerk should be familiar with the rules regarding sanctions and with the jurisprudence of the circuit court of appeals concerning their interpretation and application.

TRIAL

Frequently law clerks do not attend the trial of a case because they are engaged in activities relating to that case or to other matters that require their attention. However, a law clerk attending a trial may be called upon to perform one or more of the following duties:

1. Assist in jury selection (see pp. 98-103 for more information on jury selection and management);

2. Check the case file before trial to ensure that all necessary documents are present;

3. Serve as court crier;

4. Act as messenger as needed by the judge;

5. Take notes of the testimony;

6. Perform research on matters that arise during the course of the trial;

7. Assist in the preparation of jury instructions; and

8. In non-jury cases, assist in drafting findings of fact, conclusions of law, and judgments.

Attendance at trials is a valuable experience for a law clerk, and most judges encourage their clerks to attend interesting and skillfully presented trials when this does not interfere with their other responsibilities. A convenient alternative is for the court to have a transmitter connecting the courtroom microphones to the clerk's office so the clerk can listen when time is available.

POST-TRIAL MOTIONS

Most post-trial motions relate to attacks on the verdict or the judgment and are governed by specific provisions in the Federal Rules of Civil Procedure. Included are:

1. Motion for new trial (Rule 59);

2. Motion to alter or amend a judgment (Rule 59(e));

3. Motion for judgment notwithstanding the verdict (Rule 50(b)); and

4. Motion for relief from a judgment on the ground of:

    a. clerical mistake (Rule 60(a));

    b. other mistake (Rule 60(b));

    c. inadvertence (Rule 60(b));

    d. surprise (Rule 60(b));

    e. excusable neglect (Rule 60(b));

    f. newly discovered evidence (Rule 60(b));

    g. fraud (Rule 60(b));

    h. void judgment (Rule 60(b)); or

    i. satisfaction, release, or discharge (Rule 60(b)).

These motions are processed like pretrial motions.

Enforcement of Judgments

The procedures for execution and for supplementary proceedings in aid of judgment and execution are generally those of the state in which court is held. Fed. R. Civ. P. 69. The most common procedures are:

1. Execution;
2. Attachment;
3. Garnishment;
4. Sequestration;
5. Proceedings against sureties; and
6. Contempt proceedings.

During the course of these proceedings the court may be called upon to conduct evidentiary hearings, rule on motions, and supervise discovery in the same manner as during the original litigation on the merits.

SOCIAL SECURITY APPEALS

Some districts are presented with a large volume of appeals from the decisions of administrative agencies, and they have created special procedures to handle them. An example is petitions for review of adverse decisions of the Social Security Administration (SSA). Some judges refer these to magistrates. Others handle these cases themselves with the assistance of law clerks. Typically, these cases concern eligibility for Social Security Disability Insurance Benefits or Supplemental Security Income Benefits (SSI). The former are awarded only when a claimant with a sufficient number of quarters of insured employment has suffered such a mental or physical impairment that the claimant cannot perform substantial gainful employment for at least a year. The latter are awarded when the income and assets of a disabled person drop below a certain level and the person is not eligible for Disability Insurance Benefits.

If the SSA rejects a claim for such benefits, the claimant may obtain a hearing before an Administrative Law Judge (ALJ) at which the ALJ questions the claimant, who may be represented by counsel, and any witnesses, and examines the records and medical or financial reports furnished by the claimant or the SSA. There is no advocate for the SSA at this hearing; the ALJ serves a function similar to that of an investigating magistrate in a European court. The ALJ writes an opinion, and if the claim is denied, the claimant may appeal to the SSA Appeals Council, the final resort within the administrative system. If the Appeals Council denies a hearing or affirms the ALJ, "the decision of the Secretary" (as it is called) is final and may be appealed, within 60 days, to the district court.

District court review is statutorily limited to a deferential examination of the record to determine whether adequate procedures were followed, whether the SSA relied on correct legal standards, and whether there is substantial evidence to support the administrative decision.

After a claimant files a petition, which may be in short form, the U.S. Attorney's office supplies the court with the administrative record and an answer. Most districts have a general procedural order for the review procedure in such cases. This order requires the Assistant U.S. Attorney (AUSA) to file a motion for summary judgment to affirm the Secretary's decision. The claimant may file a reply brief within a period fixed by the local rules and the matter is then automatically taken under submission without oral argument, unless the judge orders otherwise.

Once the matter is under submission, the law clerk must write a draft order or opinion affirming the SSA (the most common result because of the limited scope of review), remanding for a new hearing because of a procedural or legal error, or to take new evidence (not infrequent), modifying the decision (rare), or reversing it (also rare).

The law clerk should obtain sample opinions rendered by the judge in other social security cases and use them as models. L. Liebman, *Disability Appeals in Social Security Programs* (Federal Judicial Center 1985) describes the Social Security Disability and Supplemental Security Income systems and the legal issues that frequently arise on judicial review of agency decisions.

APPEALS

The basic steps in the appeal of a judgment are discussed in the section on appeals beginning on p. 65.

§ 2. Bankruptcy Cases and the Bankruptcy Courts

GENERAL STRUCTURE

The district courts have original and exclusive jurisdiction of all cases under the Bankruptcy Code. Thus a bankruptcy case may be filed only in a federal district court, not a state court. The district courts also have original but not exclusive jurisdiction over "all civil proceedings arising under title 11, or arising in or related to cases under title 11." 28 U.S.C. § 1334(b). These phrases— "proceedings arising under title 11" and "arising in or related to cases under title 11"—are terms of art. The word "case" refers to the entire matter relating to a particular debtor. A "proceeding" is any disputed matter arising in the course of a "case." Thus a single case may present many proceedings. By creating the bankruptcy jurisdictional scheme, Congress intended to eliminate the litigation over jurisdiction that occurred under the former Bankruptcy Act.

The definition of the terms "arising under," "arising in," and "related to" and the distinctions between them are complex and are still being judicially defined. The most complete discussion is found in *Collier on Bankruptcy* (15th ed.). In addition there are a number of shorter and simpler books on bankruptcy, which are cited at the end of this section.

Because federal jurisdiction over civil *proceedings* is nonexclusive, other federal and state courts are not deprived of jurisdiction over matters to which bankruptcy jurisdiction extends. It is frequently desirable to permit bankruptcy litigation to proceed elsewhere even though the bankruptcy court has jurisdiction to hear it. Thus, the district court or the bankruptcy court may for various reasons choose (or may occasionally be required) to abstain from hearing a particular proceeding, may remand an action removed to it, or may authorize an action to be filed originally in some other trial court.

Federal bankruptcy jurisdiction, even when nonexclusive, is paramount. Litigation in other courts is generally stayed automatically by the filing of a bankruptcy petition, Bankruptcy Code § 362, or may be enjoined by an affirmative injunction issued under Bankruptcy Code § 105(a). Actions in other courts may be removed to the district court sitting in bankruptcy. 28 U.S.C. § 1452. The decision to abstain or to remand or not to remand a removed action is not reviewable. 28 U.S.C. §§ 1334(c)(2), 1452(b).

Abstention in a civil proceeding ordinarily is discretionary with the federal court. The standard is merely the flexible one of "interest of justice" or comity with state courts or state law. 28 U.S.C. § 1334(c)(1). When the lawsuit is a traditional matter for the civil courts or involves issues about which bankruptcy judges lack special expertise, the district court may decide to abstain, particularly if the litigation would be lengthy, the bankruptcy court's regular calendar is crowded, and a reasonably prompt disposition by the state court could be expected.

In certain limited situations, abstention is mandatory if a timely motion is made. The court must abstain if the proceeding is a "related" proceeding; it is based on a cause of action created by state law; the proceeding does not "arise in" or "arise under" title 11; an action is commenced in state court; the action can be timely adjudicated, in a state forum of appropriate jurisdiction, and there is no diversity or federal-question jurisdiction.

Each judicial district has a bankruptcy court, which constitutes a unit of the district court, 28 U.S.C. § 151, and to which it may refer bankruptcy cases and proceedings, 28 U.S.C. § 157(a). Bankruptcy judges are appointed by the circuit court for a term of 14 years and may be removed from office only for incompetence, misconduct, neglect of duty, or physical or mental disability, and then only by the circuit judicial council. If the district has more than one bankruptcy judge, judges of the district court designate which is to serve as chief judge. Each bankruptcy judge is entitled to a staff, including a secretary and a law clerk.

The bankruptcy laws are codified in two places in the U.S. Code. Title 28, the Judicial Code, contains the provisions on bankruptcy jurisdiction, the bankruptcy judges and the "bankruptcy court," venue and transfer, and the structure of the U.S. trustee system. Title 11, the Bankruptcy Code, contains both substantive and procedural law for bankruptcy proceedings. The Bankruptcy Code was adopted by the Bankruptcy Reform Act of 1978, and has been amended by: (1) the Federal Judgeship Act of 1984, the bankruptcy section of which was passed primarily to remedy constitutional defects in the Code's provisions for the jurisdiction of bankruptcy courts following the decision in Northern Pipeline Construction Co. v. Marathon Pipe Line Co., 458 U.S. 50 (1982); and (2) the Family Farmer Bankruptcy Act of 1986, 11 U.S.C. § 1201 et seq.

Appeals from the bankruptcy courts are taken to the district courts. A circuit court of appeals may establish a Bankruptcy Appeals Panel (BAP) consisting of three bankruptcy judges. If the circuit creates such a panel, and if the district court authorizes appeals from the district to go to the BAP, and if the parties consent, then the BAP may hear appeals from bankruptcy judge decisions. Further appeals from both district court and BAP decisions are taken to the circuit court of appeals.

Because appeals from bankruptcy courts are taken first to district courts (or to BAPs) and then to circuit courts, it is important for clerks for all federal courts to understand the bankruptcy court structure. Most bankruptcy practice is handled by specialists who may assume that everyone else is familiar with the bankruptcy system.

REFERENCE TO BANKRUPTCY COURT

The district court in which a case is commenced has exclusive jurisdiction of the bankruptcy case and of all property of the debtor, wherever located, as of the commencement of the case. As noted above, the district court also has concurrent jurisdiction over "proceedings" that "arise in," "arise under," or are "related to" the proceeding. Pursuant to 28 U.S.C. § 157(a), the district courts are authorized to refer to the bankruptcy judges for the district any or all cases under title 11 and all proceedings that "arise in," "arise under," or are "related to" these cases.

Each district court has a standing order referring all bankruptcy cases and proceedings to the bankruptcy court. The district court may, however, decide not to refer a specific case or proceeding or, after having referred it, may withdraw the reference.

Bankruptcy judges may enter a final order in all *"core proceedings* arising under title 11," but not in *"non-core proceedings,"* a term that simply includes all matters that are not "core" proceedings. As the phrase itself implies, "core proceeding" describes matters that are at the heart of the bankruptcy case (except that, even when they affect the assets of the estate, personal-injury and wrongful-death tort claims must be tried by the district court). The phrase is defined specifically, albeit not inclusively, in 28 U.S.C. § 157(b)(2), which contains a non-exclusive list of 15 items that are core proceedings.

The Code contains no express definition of a non-core proceeding. One example is an in personam cause of action, not created by the Code, that the debtor possessed at the time of the petition and that became a part of the estate as a result of the filing of the case. Another is a suit between third parties to which neither the debtor nor the estate is a party but which is within the broad jurisdictional grant because it indirectly affects the estate, such as a suit by a creditor against a guarantor of the debtor's obligation.

The bankruptcy judge determines initially whether a particular matter is core or not. Unless the parties by consent give the bankruptcy judge authority to enter final orders and judgments in a non-core matter, the bankruptcy judge must submit proposed findings of fact and conclusions of law in such matters to the district court. Bankruptcy judges may assign to their clerks the preparation of drafts of such findings and conclusions. After considering the bankruptcy judge's proposed findings and conclusions and after reviewing de novo those matters to which any party has timely and specifically objected, the district court enters the final judgment.

The Code relieves the bankruptcy judge of administrative and ministerial functions to allow the judge to concentrate on the performance of essentially judicial functions. Administrative matters in a bankruptcy case are performed by the office of the U.S. Trustee, as discussed below.

THE BANKRUPTCY CODE

The Code is divided into chapters, each originally odd numbered. The first three chapters contain provisions of general applicability. Chapter 1 contains definitions, rules of construction, and other general rules. Chapter 3, "Case Administration," covers how a case is begun (voluntary and involuntary petitions); deals with officers and their compensation; and contains various administrative provisions and administrative powers, including provisions concerning the automatic stay (§ 362); the use, sale, and lease of property (§ 363); and the assumption or rejection of executory contracts (§ 365). Chapter 5 contains much of the substantive bankruptcy law concerning creditors, debtors, and the estate.

The provisions of Chapters 1, 3, and 5 apply in any kind of case under the Bankruptcy Code, whether it be liquidation under Chapter 7 or rehabilitation under Chapter 11, 12, or 13. Chapter 9 contains its own section, § 901, specifying which provisions in the other chapters apply in a Chapter 9 case. In contrast, the provisions found in Chapters 7, 9, 11, 12, and 13 apply only to cases brought under their particular chapter.

Chapter 7 relates to liquidation proceedings or "straight bankruptcy." Its purpose is to achieve a fair distribution to creditors of whatever non-exempt property the debtor has and to give the individual debtor a fresh start through the discharge in bankruptcy. It requires the appointment of a trustee whose sole function is to collect and liquidate the debtor's assets in order to generate cash for distribution to creditors. If the debtor has complied with applicable law, the debtor will receive a discharge of all dischargeable debts. A creditor may, however, object to the discharge of the debtor or only to the discharge of a particular debt. The Code states the grounds on which such objections may be made. Liquidations of stockbrokers and commodity brokers are governed by a separate subchapter.

Chapter 9 relates to adjustment of the debts of a municipality and is seldom invoked.

Chapter 11, entitled "Reorganization," is the primary rehabilitation proceeding. It applies to debtors engaged in business, including individuals, partnerships, and corporations, whether publicly or closely held. The goal of Chapter 11 cases ordinarily is to rehabilitate a business as a going concern rather than to liquidate it. Unless a trustee is appointed by the court, the debtor is allowed to remain in possession (as a "debtor-in-possession" or "D-I-P") of its property. The chapter's purpose is to give the debtor a fresh start through the binding effect of an order confirming a plan of reorganization, after full disclosure to all interested persons.

Chapter 12, adopted in 1986 and scheduled to expire in 1993, is presently the only even-numbered chapter. It provides for the adjustment of the debts of a family farmer with regular income. Chapter 12 plans are similar to Chapter 13 plans rather than to Chapter 11 reorganizations. As is the situation under Chapter 13, but unlike Chapter 11, a discharge is not effective until all payments are made.

Chapter 13 is a rehabilitation provision for wage earners and other individuals with a regular income whose debts do not exceed specified amounts. Typically it is used to budget some of the debtor's future earnings under a plan through which all creditors are paid in whole or in part. The fresh start results from the discharge granted at the end of the case; the debtor's incentive to propose a plan rather than use Chapter 7 is due to the ability of the debtor to retain all property rather than turn it over to a trustee for liquidation and from the sometimes more favorable or broad discharge provisions found in Chapter 13. Chapter 13 is available only to individuals who meet the eligibility requirements set forth in § 109 of the Code.

BANKRUPTCY RULES

A case in bankruptcy court begins with the filing of a petition under the applicable chapter. If the debtor initiates the bankruptcy case, it is voluntary. Creditors, however, may initiate involuntary cases, but only under Chapters 7 and 11. The petition is filed under the specific chapter of the Code that governs the type of case contemplated. With limited exceptions, cases can generally be converted from one chapter to another.

The Rules of Bankruptcy Procedure ("RBP") govern cases in bankruptcy courts. Many of the rules are modeled on (and many even incorporate by reference) the Federal Rules of Civil Procedure. In addition, most districts have local bankruptcy rules governing some of the procedural aspects of bankruptcy cases. A clerk for a bankruptcy judge should obtain a copy of both the RBP and the local bankruptcy rules in addition to the local district court rules and keep all of these readily available.

Certain types of proceedings within bankruptcy cases are called "adversary proceedings" and these are governed and defined by RBP 7001 et seq. All matters in a bankruptcy case that do not qualify as adversary proceedings are called "contested matters."

The summons issued by the bankruptcy court clerk sets a date for either a trial or pretrial conference when a complaint in an adversary proceeding within a bankruptcy case is filed. Contested matters are commenced by the filing of a motion. Local practice (usually set out in local rules) determines how motions are set for hearings. First class mail is usually used for service in adversary proceedings and contested matters. The rules regarding pleadings and discovery are similar to those in the Federal Rules of Civil Procedure.

When a bankruptcy petition is filed, all judicial proceedings in which the debtor is involved are automatically stayed. Thereafter a variety of motions may be filed seeking some relief from the court. This will usually be granted after notice to other parties in interest if no one raises an objection. A typical motion is a motion for the abandonment of burdensome property.

A clerk for a bankruptcy judge may be assigned the same tasks in connection with motions, whether ex parte or contested, that are assigned to clerks for district courts. See pp. 29-32. The functions of the bankruptcy judges' clerks in the trial of adversary proceedings are the same as those of district court clerks in civil cases. See pp. 39-40.

U.S. TRUSTEES

The office of the U.S. Trustee handles the administrative functions of bankruptcy courts. Following an experimental program using U.S. Trustees, Congress in 1986 adopted the program nationwide. The Bankruptcy Amendments Act of 1986 divided the United States into 21 geographic regions, in each of which a U.S.

Trustee is responsible for bankruptcy administration. 25 U.S.C. § 581(a). Although in most regions the program has already been implemented, it may not become effective nationwide until 1991. The U.S. Trustee performs these functions:

1. Establishes, maintains, and supervises a panel of private trustees to serve in cases under Chapter 7. 28 U.S.C. § 586(a)(1).

2. Serves as a trustee in a Chapter 11 case when required to do so by that chapter. 28 U.S.C. § 586(a)(2).

3. Supervises the administration of cases and trustees. 28 U.S.C. § 586(a)(3).

4. Deposits or invests money received as trustee pursuant to § 345 of the Bankruptcy Code.

5. Performs the duties prescribed for the U.S. Trustee under title 11.

6. Makes such reports as the Attorney General directs.

PRIVATE TRUSTEES

Private trustees are individuals appointed in a specific case to carry out the duties of a trustee in that case. Each judicial district has, with the approval of the Administrative Office, designated a number of persons with competence in bankruptcy matters to serve as trustees.

In a Chapter 7 case, when the petition is filed, the U.S. Trustee appoints a disinterested person from the panel of private trustees to serve as interim trustee. In an involuntary case, if the court orders the appointment of an interim trustee before the entry of the order for relief, the U.S. Trustee makes the appointment. At the first meeting of creditors, creditors may elect another person as trustee, although such elections are rare.

In a Chapter 11 case, no trustee is appointed unless the court orders the appointment after notice and a hearing. If the court orders the appointment of a trustee, the U.S. Trustee designates the person who will serve.

In Chapter 12 and Chapter 13 cases, a standing trustee (selected by the U.S. Trustee) serves in all cases; in a few districts there are several standing Chapter 12 or Chapter 13 trustees.

THE CLERK OF BANKRUPTCY COURT

In almost all districts, the administration of the bankruptcy court is directed by a separate clerk. In a few districts, however, the clerk of the district court also serves as clerk of the bankruptcy court. The functions of the bankruptcy clerk's office are similar to those of the clerk of the district court.

SUGGESTED SUPPLEMENTAL READING

Collier on Bankruptcy (15th ed.), a 13-volume treatise

W. Drake, Jr., and A. Mullens, Jr., *Bankruptcy Practice for the General Practitioner* (1978)

H. Liebowitz, *Bankruptcy Deskbook* (1986)

G. Triester, J. Trost, L. Forman, K. Klee, and R. Levin, *Fundamentals of Bankruptcy Law* (1986)

Note also: Clerks to bankruptcy judges and district judges may wish to borrow the Federal Judicial Center video orientation lectures for bankruptcy judges. These 14 lectures by sitting bankruptcy judges cover procedures in the bankruptcy courts, the courts' organization and jurisdiction, and the essential substantive provisions of Chapters 11, 12, and 13.

§ 3. The Criminal Action

In federal law there are no common-law crimes, only statutory offenses. Most federal crimes are defined in title 18 of the U.S. Code, but some criminal penalties are set forth in various other specific statutes. The procedure in criminal cases is governed by the Federal Rules of Criminal Procedure and, in misdemeanor cases, by the Misdemeanor Rules. Much of the law clerk's involvement in criminal cases is similar to that described earlier for civil cases.

The following materials outline the major steps that take place in a criminal case. This outline is only a generalization to aid in understanding the process. Individual cases may proceed in a different manner, and the case may terminate at various stages, such as when a guilty plea is entered by the defendant or when the court grants a motion to dismiss the indictment or the jury finds the defendant not guilty.

PROCEEDINGS BEFORE A MAGISTRATE

A criminal case may begin in any of the following ways:

1. Arrest without warrant followed by:

   a. filing of a complaint (Fed. R. Crim. P. 3);

   b. appearance before a magistrate (Rule 5);

   c. commitment or release on bail (18 U.S.C. §§ 3142, 3144);

   d. preliminary hearing before a magistrate (Rule 5.1); and

   e. grand jury presentment (Rule 6).

2. Arrest on warrant issued upon a complaint (Rule 3) followed by:

   a. appearance before a magistrate;

   b. commitment or release on bail;

   c. preliminary hearing before a magistrate; and

   d. grand jury indictment (Rule 6).

3. Arrest on warrant issued upon indictment (Rule 6) followed by:

   a. appearance before a magistrate; and

   b. commitment or release on bail.

4. Issuance of summons (Rule 9), which directs the defendant to appear without being arrested.

Upon arrest a defendant must be brought before a magistrate "without unnecessary delay." Fed. R. Crim. P. 5 requires that, at the first appearance before the magistrate, the defendant must be advised of:

1. The charges contained in the complaint or the indictment and the content of any affidavits filed with the complaint;

2. The right to counsel;

3. The right to have counsel appointed if the defendant is financially unable to retain counsel;

4. The right to a preliminary hearing;

5. The fact that the defendant is not required to make a statement and that, if the defendant does so, it may be used against the defendant.

The magistrate may take the following additional actions:

1. If the defendant cannot afford to retain counsel, appoint counsel unless the defendant declines the assistance of counsel (18 U.S.C. § 3006A(b));

2. Determine bail or other conditions for release (18 U.S.C.§ 3142); and

3. If the defendant is unable to post bail or meet the conditions for release established by the magistrate, commit the defendant to custody (18 U.S.C.§ 3142(e)).

The purpose of the preliminary hearing before a magistrate is to determine whether there is probable cause to believe that an offense has been committed and that the defendant has committed it. If the magistrate finds there is such probable cause, the defendant is held for further proceedings in the district court. If the magistrate finds a lack of probable cause, the defendant is discharged. Rule 5.1.

At the preliminary hearing the defendant may cross-examine witnesses and may introduce evidence. The defendant may waive a preliminary hearing, and is then held for further proceedings in the district court.

INDICTMENT

The Fifth Amendment guarantees a person charged with a serious federal crime the right to have the charge presented to a grand jury.

Grand juries are empanelled by the district court as needed. A grand jury consists of not less than 16 nor more than 23 members who are selected in accordance with the jury selection plan of the district court. Fed. R. Crim. P. 6. The jury continues to serve until discharged by the court, but it may not serve for more than 18 months.

Rule 6(c) states that the court "shall appoint one of the jurors to be foreperson and another to be deputy foreperson." The foreperson is responsible for recording the number of jurors concurring in the finding on each indictment and for filing that record with the clerk of court.

Grand jury proceedings are usually secret unless, in a particular case, the court directs disclosure. Fed. R. Crim. P. 6(e). Government counsel, the witness, and necessary court reporters and interpreters may be present while evidence is being presented, but only the jurors themselves may be present during deliberation and voting.

A defendant who is entitled to be prosecuted by indictment may waive that right in open court. If so, prosecution is by bill of information. Fed. R. Crim. P. 7.

ARRAIGNMENT

The purpose of arraignment is to frame the issues between the prosecution and the defense. The defendant may plead guilty, not guilty, or nolo contendere. The court may refuse to accept a plea of guilty or nolo contendere. If the defendant pleads guilty or nolo contendere, the court must be satisfied that the defendant understands the nature of the charge, the maximum possible penalty, the minimum mandatory penalty, if any, and that the plea is made voluntarily. Fed. R. Crim. P. 11(a). Some judges also ask questions to satisfy themselves that defendants accused of crimes committed after October 1987 understand that the Sentencing Reform Act applies and that, therefore, the sentencing guidelines will likely be used to determine the sentence. (For more information on sentencing, see p. 59.) At the time of arraignment, however, the defendant will usually plead not guilty. This gives counsel time to research the legal rules governing the charges, investigate the evidence against the client, ascertain whether any of the evidence may be suppressed, and determine whether a plea bargain is desirable or possible.

Thereafter a plea of guilty or nolo contendere is frequently entered as a result of plea bargaining between the prosecution and the defense. Plea bargaining is a process through which the defendant agrees to enter a guilty plea on the condition that the prosecution reduce the charge, dismiss some of a group of multiple charges, or grant some other concession of benefit to the defendant. The judge must inquire of a defendant whether there has been any agreement or plea bargain and, if so, the understanding or agreement must be fully set forth in the record. Fed. R. Crim. P. 11(e). In the federal court system the judge is not a party to the plea bargaining process and is not bound by any agreement made between the defendant and the government. For defendants subject to the Sentencing Guidelines, judges may accept the plea on a conditional basis, pending determination of the guideline sentence. Only with that determination can the court know whether the sentence contemplated by the plea agreement accords with the sentence allowed under the guidelines.

If the defendant pleads not guilty and does not thereafter change the plea, the case proceeds to trial.

PRETRIAL MOTIONS

The motions most frequently filed before trial:

1. Challenge the sufficiency of the indictment or information, by way of a motion to dismiss;

2. Challenge the jurisdiction or venue;

3. Seek to suppress evidence, usually on the basis that it has been obtained in a manner that violated the defendant's constitutional rights;

4. Seek to discover evidence;

5. When the defendant is indigent:

   a. request that specialized services such as psychiatric examination, special investigations, or expert services be provided at the expense of the United States;

   b. obtain the appointment of counsel if this has not already been done; and

6. Seek to obtain the release of the defendant on reduced bail or the defendant's own recognizance while awaiting trial.

Motions may be filed late. For example, a motion for severance of a trial from the trial of a codefendant may be filed three or four days before the pretrial conference, which itself may be set only a week or two before trial. The Assistant U.S. Attorney (AUSA) charged with the prosecution of the case may not respond until the pretrial conference. When, therefore, a motion is filed in a criminal case, it usually requires prompt attention, and often the clerk will brief the judge verbally or write a memo summarizing the motion and the law on the subject before the opposition papers are filed.

DISCOVERY AND PRETRIAL OMNIBUS HEARING

Traditionally, discovery in criminal cases has been extremely limited. However, Fed. R. Crim. P. 16 permits the defendant to discover some of the evidentiary material in the government's hands. If the defendant does seek discovery under Rule 16, the government is entitled to a limited amount of discovery in return. The matters that are subject to such discovery are set forth specifically in that rule.

Many courts conduct a hearing before trial for the purpose of determining what motions will be filed, simplifying issues, and expediting as far as possible the full and complete disclosure of evidence. This so-called omnibus hearing is designed to combine all discovery procedures and all motions. Proponents of these hearings state that they assure that the defendant has asserted all possible rights and defenses, avoid last-minute motions, streamline the trial, and eliminate a certain number of trials that would have been conducted only because counsel were unaware of the evidence to be presented by the government. Some districts refer to the hearing by the number of the local rule concerning it, for example, a Rule 2.04 hearing. The clerk should inquire whether the court has such a rule and, if so, should become familiar with it.

TRIAL AND POST-TRIAL DETENTION

The jury in a criminal case consists of 12 jurors and as many alternates as the court thinks necessary. At trial, the jury is empanelled, evidence is presented, and a verdict is rendered by the jury. If the verdict is "guilty," the court must decide whether to alter the custody of the defendant pending sentencing and must set a date to impose sentence. If the defendant is not in custody, the judge will usually inquire whether the defendant should be at large on the same bond, pending imposition of sentence. The Bail Reform

Act of 1984 requires that a person who has been found guilty and who is awaiting imposition of sentence be detained unless the judge finds "by clear and convincing evidence that the person is not likely to flee or pose a danger to the safety of any other person or the community" if released. 18 U.S.C. § 3143(a). A presentence investigation will usually be ordered. The defendant is either notified to appear for sentencing on a fixed date, or is informed that the court will give notice by mail of the date when sentence is to be imposed.

THE SPEEDY TRIAL ACT

According to its preamble, Congress enacted the Speedy Trial Act of 1974 (18 U.S.C. §§ 3152–56, 3161–74, and 28 U.S.C. § 604(a)(9)) "to assist in reducing crime and the danger of recidivism by requiring speedy trials and by strengthening the supervision over persons released pending trial." Title I of that Act has an important impact on proceedings in criminal cases. It requires each district to adopt a plan for the disposition of criminal cases. The law clerk should become thoroughly familiar both with the Act and the local court plan.

The administration of the criminal trial calendar is vested in the court. The Act requires the court "at the earliest practicable time . . . after consultation with the counsel for the defendant and the attorney for the Government" to set the case for trial "on a day certain, or list it for trial on a weekly or other short-term trial calendar." 18 U.S.C. § 3161(a).

The prosecutor must file an information or indictment within 30 days of arrest or service of summons. 18 U.S.C. § 3161(b). An additional 30 days is allowed if no grand jury has met in the district within the first 30-day period.

Then commences an inexorable movement toward trial. Further time limits are prescribed in § 3161.

There are eight exclusions for delays that will not violate speedy trial requirements. These include:

1. Mental or physical examination, § 3161(h)(1)(A);
2. Hearings on pretrial motions, § 3161(h)(1)(F);

3. Period not to exceed 30 days during which the judge has a matter concerning the defendant under advisement, § 3161(h)(1)(J);

4. Period during which prosecution is deferred by written agreement with the defendant, with the approval of the court, for the purpose of allowing the defendant to demonstrate his good conduct, § 3161(h)(2);

5. Periods when the defendant or an essential witness is absent or unavailable or is mentally incapable, § 3161(h)(3)(A), (h)(4); and

6. Delay resulting from a continuance issued by a judge on the court's own motion or that of counsel, if the continuance was granted based on the judge's findings that the ends of justice served by the delay outweighed the public and defense interest in a speedy trial, § 3161(h)(8)(A).

No continuance can be granted because of court congestion or lack of diligent preparation or failure to obtain witnesses on the part of the government.

Failure to meet prescribed time limits requires dismissal of the charge. 18 U.S.C. § 3162. Whether the dismissal is with or without prejudice is to be determined by the court after considering the:

1. Seriousness of the offense;

2. Facts and circumstances of the case that led to dismissal; and

3. Impact of a reprosecution on the administration of the Act and on the administration of justice.

The Act provides sanctions for counsel, both for the defendant and for the government, if counsel:

1. Knowingly allows a case to be set for trial without disclosing the unavailability of a necessary witness;

2. Files a motion solely for the purpose of delay which counsel knows is totally frivolous and without merit;

3. Knowingly makes a materially false statement to obtain a continuance; or

4. Otherwise willfully fails to proceed with trial without justification.

The maximum penalties are fixed by the Act.

SENTENCING

(*Note:* This material applies to offenses committed on or after November 1, 1987, the effective date of the sentencing guidelines described below. Offenses committed before November 1, 1987, are not subject to guideline sentencing, and the judge has considerably more discretion as to the sentence to impose. The presentence report prepared for such offenses will be much different from the report described below.)

Sources

Sentencing and sentencing procedures in federal court are controlled by four main sources: the statutory maximums and minimums prescribed for the offenses in title 18 and other sections of the U.S. Code; the Sentencing Reform Act of 1984, and various subsequent amending statutes; the *Sentencing Guidelines and Policy Statements* and amendments issued by the U.S. Sentencing Commission pursuant to the Sentencing Reform Act; and the Federal Rules of Criminal Procedure, especially Rule 32 ("Sentence and Judgment") and Rule 35 ("Correction of Sentence").

Each judge's chambers has a copy of the Commission's *Sentencing Guidelines and Policy Statements*. An appendix to this document includes the sections of titles 18 and 28 enacted by the Sentencing Reform Act (note, however, that this is not an authoritative version of the legislation). Later statutory amendments distributed by the Administrative Office, as well as guideline amendments issued by the Commission, should be inserted in the guidelines binder for ease of reference. Clerks may also wish to consult the Federal Judicial Center's *Guideline Sentencing Orientation* manual, a loose-leaf document prepared in 1987. The manual includes annotated exercises that illustrate the essential points of guideline application for the initial (April 1987) version of the guidelines; the clerk should be certain, however, to consult any subsequent statutory or guideline amendments, which may affect the specific results in the exercises. Other instructional material that the Center or the Commission may distribute should be kept with the guidelines manual or the orientation manual for reference.

Guideline Sentencing

In the 1984 Sentencing Reform Act, Congress attempted to reduce unwarranted disparity in sentencing and ensure that similar defendants who commit similar crimes receive similar sentences. It also attempted to ensure that defendants serve the sentence imposed by the court rather than have the actual sentence determined by a parole commission. Consequently, Congress created the U.S. Sentencing Commission as a permanent agency in the judicial branch and directed it to promulgate sentencing guidelines and amendments to the guidelines, which take effect absent congressional action.

The Sentencing Reform Act also authorized the Commission to issue "policy statements," to explain the guidelines and their application. The Commission has also provided "commentary" in its guidelines document, which further explains the guidelines and the Commission's intent. Only the sentencing *guidelines,* however—strictly defined and identified as such in the guidelines document—have the force of law. The Sentencing Reform Act directs the sentencing court to "consider" the policy statements in imposing sentence (18 U.S.C. § 3553(a)(5)). At the time of sentencing the court must state in open court the reasons for its imposition of the particular sentence. If it imposes a sentence "not of the kind" or "outside the range" prescribed by the guidelines, the court must state "the specific reason for the imposition of a sentence different" from the one prescribed by the guidelines. 18 U.S.C. § 3553(c). Either the defendant or the government may appeal a sentence imposed as a result of an incorrect application of the guidelines (but not of the policy statements). 18 U.S.C. § 3742.

Pursuant to the Sentencing Reform Act, the Commission has established numerous categories of offense conduct, to which it has assigned levels according to the seriousness of the offense. The levels are to be adjusted based on particular characteristics of the offense (such as use of a weapon), so that the sentence reflects the "total offense conduct," not simply the offense charged in the indictment. Also pursuant to statute, the Commission has established various categories of defendants, based on their criminal history. And it has prescribed a sentencing range, in months, for each combination of offense level and criminal history category.

The judge must impose a sentence within the range prescribed by the guidelines unless "the court finds that there exists an aggravating or mitigating circumstance of a kind, or to a degree, that was not adequately taken into consideration by the Sentencing Commission in formulating the guidelines that should result in a sentence different from that described." In making a finding about what the Commission considered, the court, by statute, may "consider only the sentencing guidelines, policy statements, and official commentary of the Sentencing Commission." 18 U.S.C. § 3553(b). If it does make such a finding, the court may depart from the sentence prescribed by the guidelines.

The sentence imposed will be the length of time actually to be served, except that 54 days of good time credit may be earned each year after the first year. The guidelines also tell how to determine the fine to be imposed in addition to any statutorily required restitution. And they indicate when probation or some other sentence instead of incarceration may be imposed. Although the Sentencing Reform Act does not provide for parole, the sentence may include a term of supervised release to follow the prison sentence.

Sentencing Procedures

In most courts, the basic document the judge uses to determine the sentence is the presentence report prepared by the probation officer assigned to the case. Fed. R. Crim. P. 32(c)(2) prescribes the contents of the presentence report. The report presents the facts of the case relevant to guideline sentencing, explains the results of the application of the guidelines to them, and provides the officer's confidential sentencing recommendation. It may contain an addendum listing statements in the report to which one of the parties objects, and the officer's comments on those objections. The Probation Division of the Administrative Office has suggested a standard format for presentence reports and has prepared a document explaining it. The court's probation office can provide general information about the report and its preparation.

18 U.S.C. § 3552(d) requires that the presentence report be disclosed to the defendant at least 10 days before sentencing. A number of courts have local rules that provide for disclosure of the presentence report 20 or even more days in advance of sentencing. The purpose of this longer time period is to allow the attorneys to review the report and discuss their objections with the probation officer. The probation officer can revise the report to take account of legitimate objections and summarize and then comment upon unresolved objections in an addendum to the revised presentence report. Some courts have adopted local rules that do not inject the probation officer so extensively into the fact-finding process. They direct the parties to file a motion or memorandum discussing unresolved issues directly with the court.

If there are disputed factual issues that would affect the sentence, the judge may find it necessary to hold an evidentiary hearing before imposing sentence. The Federal Rules of Evidence do not apply at the sentencing hearing. In addition, if there is a dispute concerning the correct interpretation of the guidelines, the court may wish to hear argument from the attorneys. After resolving the matters in dispute, the judge imposes sentence. 18 U.S.C. § 3553(c) requires the court to state the reasons for the sentence on the record to facilitate appellate review. It also requires that a statement of reasons be furnished to the probation office and, if the sentence includes imprisonment, to the Bureau of Prisons.

Appellate Review

Either the defendant or the government may appeal the sentence if it was imposed in violation of law or represents an incorrect application of the guidelines. Also, guideline departures are appealable by the defendant if the sentence is above the guidelines, or by the government if it is below. The standard for review is reasonableness. If the appeals court reverses the sentence, the case is remanded to the district court for resentencing. Fed. R. Crim. P. 35 requires the court, upon remand, to correct a sentence determined on appeal to have been improperly imposed, but the rule, as amended in 1985, no longer gives the judge authority in other circumstances to reopen the sentence, even if it is illegal, except that the government may petition for a reduction in reward for cooperation.

Role of Clerks

District judges will vary as to what they require of their clerks in respect to sentencing. Clerks who are asked to review the presentence report to assess the correctness of the probation officer's guidelines application will have to become thoroughly familiar with the Commission's *Sentencing Guidelines and Policy Statements;* the guidelines, policy statements, and commentary can be quite complex, and sometimes yield more than one plausible interpretation. Simply consulting the guideline for the type of offense in question will rarely produce a correct offense level determination. A correct determination will also reflect, for example, how much of the offender's actual conduct should be taken into account in applying the specific offense characteristics. One must, moreover, be familiar with the entire structure of the guidelines in order to apply them to any particular case. A properly executed presentence report will illustrate these application principles; model PSRs can be found in the Center's *Guideline Sentencing Orientation* binder at tab H.

The clerk should pay special attention also to the effective dates for the relevant legislative and guideline provisions, to ascertain which provisions apply to the offense in questions.

Some judges may also wish their clerks to draft a tentative statement of reasons for the sentence. Bear in mind that the sentence, and thus the statement of reasons, may depend on the resolution of disputed issues of law or fact; these issues may appear in the addendum to the presentence report or may be raised at the sentencing hearing.

Just before the sentencing date, the clerk should assemble the court files needed for the sentencings set on that day. These should be placed in a convenient place in chambers so that the judge may reexamine the files just before the sentencing hearing if the judge chooses to do so. They should be placed on the bench just before court is called to order.

POST-TRIAL MOTIONS

The usual post-trial motions in a criminal case are for a new trial, for arrest of judgment, or to correct or reduce the sentence. As discussed in Chapter 4, defendants will also file motions to correct or reduce their sentences, although the court's authority to correct or reduce the sentence is limited under Fed. R. Crim. P. 35. Motions under 28 U.S.C. § 2255, however, are not affected by the Act and are discussed in the next section. Post-trial motions are generally processed in the same manner as other motions.

HANDLING PRISONER PETITIONS

Federal courts receive many petitions from inmates of institutions requesting relief from their sentences. The majority are from state prisoners alleging violation by state officials of the prisoner's federally protected rights, and seeking release from state custody under the federal habeas corpus act, 28 U.S.C. § 2254. These are to be distinguished from petitions seeking damages or injunctive relief for violation of a prisoner's civil rights under 42 U.S.C. § 1983. Both § 2254 and § 1983 proceedings are civil in nature and their handling is discussed immediately below and at p. 159.

Federal prisoners may seek release from custody under 28 U.S.C. § 2255. Although § 2255 is similar to habeas corpus, it requires the petition to be filed in the sentencing court rather than in the court having jurisdiction over the place of incarceration (a § 2255 proceeding is now a continuation of the original criminal action). This eliminates problems of transferring case files and usually permits ready access to witnesses and other evidence.

Prisoner petitions are frequently handwritten and inartfully drafted. As a result they may be difficult to read and understand. The rules governing cases under § 2254 and § 2255 are available in pamphlet form from the Administrative Office and may be found in the *United States Code Annotated* following the statutory sections. Pro se petitioners in such cases must complete a standard form in order to make the facts alleged and the nature of the claim more intelligible. The forms now available are:

AO-241—Form for Use in Applications for Habeas Corpus Under 28 U.S.C. § 2254

AO-242—Form for Use in 28 U.S.C. § 2254 Cases Involving a Rule 9 Issue

AO-244—Form for Motions Under 28 U.S.C. § 2255 Cases Involving a Rule 9 Issue.

These forms are mandatory in pro se cases, but district courts may amend them to meet local requirements. They assist prisoners and the court by ensuring that critical information is provided in a coherent format. In a further attempt to process the large volume of prisoner petitions, some courts have created the position of motions clerk or pro se clerk to assist with them. Some district courts also have standard forms for use as pro se petitions based on § 1983. (Additional discussion of prisoner correspondence can be found at p. 154.)

The disposition of many of the post-conviction petitions can be decided from an examination of the papers themselves, but if material factual issues are raised the court must conduct an evidentiary hearing.

§ 4. Appeals

PROCESSING APPEALS

There are fewer steps in the appellate process than in the trial process. The steps in an appeal are as follows:

1. Filing notice of appeal;
2. Preparing the record on appeal;
3. Docketing the appeal;
4. Filing of appellant's brief;
5. Filing of appellee's brief;
6. Filing of appellant's reply brief;
7. Decision by the court if it dispenses with oral argument or scheduling of oral argument;
8. Oral argument;
9. Deliberation by court;

10. Filing of opinion;

11. Filing of petition for rehearing; and

12. Issuance of mandate. (The mandate is the final stage in the appellate process unless the defendant applies to the Supreme Court for a writ of certiorari or files an appeal in those few instances in which appeals are still permitted. See, e.g., 28 U.S.C. §§ 1252, 1253, 1257.)

The Federal Rules of Appellate Procedure establish a substantial degree of procedural uniformity among the 13 circuit courts of appeals. There are still, however, some differences in the procedures of the various circuits. Each circuit has local rules and internal operating procedures that describe the precise procedure to be followed when there is any variation from the Rules and, in some instances, elaborate on or amplify the Rules. (See Chapter 4, § 7, "Case Management: The Appellate Court.")

NOTICE OF APPEAL

The timely filing of a notice of appeal is a jurisdictional requirement for any appeal. The purpose of the notice is to inform opposing counsel and the court that an appeal is being taken. The time for filing commences with the entry of the judgment or order in the district court from which the appeal is taken. The running of that time is tolled by the filing of certain post-trial motions in the district court, and the filing of such motions after a notice of appeal has been filed may vitiate the notice, requiring a new notice of appeal to be filed after the motion is decided. Fed. R. App. P. 4(a).

Rule 4 provides these time periods for filing notices of appeal:

1. Private civil cases—30 days;

2. Civil cases in which the United States is a party—60 days;

3. Criminal cases—10 days; and

4. Criminal cases in which appeal by the government is authorized by statute (such as appeals from sentences under the 1984 Sentencing Reform Act)—30 days.

The notice of appeal must be filed in the district court. The clerk of that court is required by Fed. R. App. P. 3(d) to forward a copy of the notice to the clerk of the court of appeals.

Upon receipt of the notice of appeal, most courts of appeals take steps to ensure that all procedural requirements have been met and then continue to monitor the appeal as it progresses in the district court. In some courts conferences are held with counsel shortly after the notice is filed to establish schedules for record preparation and briefing, to discuss the issues in the case with a view to eliminating the briefing of frivolous issues, and, in civil cases, to discuss the possibility of settlement. About half the circuits now require preargument conferences but their goals and procedures vary considerably.

RECORD PREPARATION

For an appellate court to review intelligently the proceedings in a trial court, the appellate judges must have a complete record of what occurred in the trial court. The appellant is required to cause a record on appeal to be filed. This consists of all the original papers and exhibits filed in the trial court plus a reporter's transcript of any relevant proceedings. The Sentencing Reform Act, 18 U.S.C. § 3742, requires that the record in a criminal case must also include "(1) that portion of the record . . . that is designated as pertinent by either of the parties; (2) the presentence report; and (3) the information submitted during the sentencing proceeding." (This information will usually be under seal, because it is confidential.)

The appellant has 40 days in which to cause the record on appeal to be sent from the district court to the court of appeals. During this time the appellant must order a transcript of proceedings if one is needed and make arrangements to pay the court reporter for services or, in courts using electronic sound recording for the official record, the clerk of court. The district court clerk assembles the other papers that constitute the record on appeal.

The district court has the power to extend for an additional 50 days the time for preparing and sending the record on appeal, after which time the court of appeals itself may grant further extensions. Additional time may be needed if the court reporter has not completed transcribing the proceedings or if counsel has failed to order the transcript timely.

To prevent undue delay, the appellate courts are generally averse to granting time extensions and may impose sanctions on the appellant or the reporter for unreasonable delays in preparing the record on appeal.

DOCKETING THE APPEAL

When the record is completed, or earlier if desired, the appellant must docket the appeal. This is primarily a clerical process and is performed in the office of the clerk of the court of appeals. Unless the appellant is exempt from payment, a docket fee is charged. The clerk of court opens an appropriate file and record and sends a notice to the parties. Frequently, docketing takes place when the record on appeal is filed.

The filing of the record provides the base date for most subsequent proceedings in the case.

BRIEFS AND JOINT APPENDIX

Each party is given an opportunity to present legal and factual arguments to the court in writing. The document through which arguments are presented is the brief. Because the appellant has the burden of persuading the court of appeals that the trial court erred, the appellant files the opening brief. The appellee then files a brief in response; and, if the appellant wishes, a reply brief may then be filed responding to any new matters raised in the appellee's brief. The Federal Rules of Appellate Procedure establish standards for format, color of brief covers, content, methods of reproduction, number of copies, and times for filing of briefs. The local rules for a circuit may impose further rules regarding the brief. The schedule for filing briefs is as follows:

1. Appellant's brief—40 days after filing the record;
2. Appellee's brief—30 days after service of appellant's brief;
3. Reply brief—14 days after service of appellee's brief.

Some courts of appeals have modified the requirements and standards of the federal rules in certain cases or classes of cases. One of the more common modifications is to permit those appealing in forma pauperis to file fewer copies of their briefs.

While the briefs are being prepared, the parties are required to determine which portions of the record on appeal are relevant to the issues raised; the appellant must then have those portions reproduced as an appendix to the briefs. Since there is only one appendix containing the portions relied upon by both the appellant and the appellee, it is referred to as a "joint appendix." If any relevant material is omitted from the appendix, the court is free to refer to the original record. Multiple copies of the appendix are filed so that each judge may have one and, if needed, each law clerk may have one. Some courts of appeals have eliminated the requirement of an appendix and permit the substitution of photocopies of a relatively few parts of the record, usually called record excerpts. The local rules of those courts describe the substitute requirements.

ORAL ARGUMENT

If the court does not, by screening the case, decide it without oral argument, the parties are given an opportunity to present their arguments to the court orally. Most cases are heard by a panel of three judges but, in order to secure or maintain uniformity of decisions or in cases involving a question of exceptional importance, a case may be heard en banc, that is, by all of the active judges on the court and any senior judge of the circuit who sat on the panel that originally heard the case (or, in the Ninth Circuit, by a "limited en banc," consisting of the Chief Judge and 10 additional judges selected by lot). En banc hearings are held only when ordered by a majority of the active judges on the court.

Fed. R. App. P. 34 permits the court to fix the time allowed for oral argument. Most courts allow 20 minutes to each side, but some reduce this amount of time for cases that the panel thinks require less time. All allow counsel to file a request in advance for additional time but such requests are not usually favored. Usually, not more than two attorneys are permitted to argue for each side. Some court rules, such as Rule 11(a) of the local rules of the Seventh Circuit, encourage argument by only one attorney for each party.

Many circuit judges require their law clerks to prepare a memorandum on each case (called a "bench memo") for the judge to review before hearing oral arguments. In some circuits, the clerk for one judge may prepare a memorandum to be circulated among the three judges prior to oral argument. Most judges will study the briefs in advance of oral argument.

The appellant begins the argument. Because the judges have read the briefs, and are therefore familiar with the issues, the judges may begin questioning the attorney shortly after the argument begins. After the appellant's argument is completed, the appellee responds, followed by any reply by the appellant.

Although the arguments are recorded so that the judges and their clerks may later review them, some circuit judges require one of their law clerks to attend oral argument and take notes of important matters, citations of new authority, and concessions made during the argument.

Some courts, such as the Second Circuit, hold hearings in only one location within the circuit, while others, such as the Ninth, still "ride circuit" and hold court in a number of locations.

DELIBERATION

After a case has been argued and submitted to the court, the panel of judges who heard the argument meets to arrive at a decision. In most courts these meetings are held immediately after each day's arguments have been completed, but in the Second Circuit the judges do not confer about a case until each member of the panel has prepared and circulated a memorandum setting forth that judge's individual views.

In the process of deciding individual cases, an appellate court performs at least three distinct functions. First, it decides the controversy before it; second, it supervises the courts within its jurisdiction; and third, it determines the growth and development of the common law and the interpretation of federal statutory and constitutional law within its jurisdiction. Each of these functions becomes important during the decisional phase of an appeal, because the court must not only reach the correct result but must also explain the rationale for that decision in its opinion.

In most cases the court arrives at a tentative agreement about the decision at the first meeting. At that time, the presiding judge of the panel (the senior active circuit judge sitting on the panel) assigns the case to one member of the panel, who later writes an opinion to be submitted to the others for approval. When agreement is not reached so readily, the members of the panel may exchange memoranda about the case and schedule additional meetings or telephone conferences for further discussion.

If a tentative agreement is not reached at the first conference, the law clerk may be called upon to write a memorandum for the judge on particular issues or the entire case; to review memoranda from other judges in order to discuss them with the judge; to perform research; and perhaps even to write a draft opinion for consideration by the judge.

OPINION AND JUDGMENT

The final product of the court in most appeals is a written opinion setting forth the decision and the reasons for that decision. The increased number of cases and the burden of writing formal opinions in every one has caused appellate courts to use alternatives to formal opinions in many cases, such as those that involve only the application of settled principles to a specific fact situation. Several kinds of opinions, therefore, may be filed:

1. *Authored*—An opinion that reports the name of the judge who prepared it in addition to names of the other members of the panel. Such an opinion is the conventional type reported in law school casebooks. It discusses the facts, the legal issues, the authorities, and the *ratio decidendi*.

2. *Per curiam*—Usually a short opinion dealing with a simple case involving issues that have been decided frequently. The opinion does not reflect the name of the judge who wrote it, but merely the names of the judges on the panel.

3. *Dissenting*—The opinion of one or more members of a panel disagreeing with the result reached by the majority.

4. *Concurring*—The opinion of one or more members of a panel, but less than a majority, agreeing with the result of the majority opinion, but not with the reasoning.

5. *Memorandum or order*—An opinion that is designed only to explain briefly to the parties the basic reasons why the panel decided the case the way it did. Such opinions are usually not published.

6. *Summary*—A brief statement that the district court judgment is affirmed or reversed.

Most circuits now have local rules or policies that guide the members of the court in deciding which cases deserve full opinions and which opinions should be published. In 1985, 16,369 appellate cases were terminated on the merits, but written, signed opinions were rendered in only 7,108—about 43 percent. Written, unsigned opinions that stated the rules of the law, explained their application to the facts of the case, and gave the judicial reasons on which the judgment was based were rendered in 7,431 cases—about 45 percent. Written unsigned opinions stating a result were rendered in 1,749 cases—about 10 percent. In a handful of cases (81), decision was announced orally. D. Stienstra, *Unpublished Dispositions: Problems of Access and Use in the Courts of Appeals* (Federal Judicial Center 1985) discusses the use of unpublished opinions. (See p. 111 regarding the distribution of opinions.)

When a panel has agreed upon an opinion, it is initialed or signed by all three judges and forwarded to the clerk of court. In some courts, opinions to be published (and perhaps others) are circulated to all active judges on the court with a time limit for noting any suggestions or revisions.

REHEARING

The party who loses an appeal may file a petition for rehearing within 14 days after judgment is entered. That petition attempts to persuade the panel that the decision was erroneous and should be withdrawn or revised. The prevailing party may not file a response to the petition unless one is requested by the court. Most petitions for rehearing are denied.

The losing party may also move for a rehearing en banc. That motion is circulated to all the members of the original panel and all active judges who did not sit on the panel. Only the active circuit judges, and any senior judge who was a member of the original panel, may request a vote on the suggestion to rehear the appeal en banc; only the active circuit judges may vote on whether the appeal should be reheard en banc; and, if a rehearing en banc is granted, only active circuit judges and senior circuit judges from the circuit who were members of the original panel may sit on the rehearing. By local rule, a circuit may impose time limitations within which a member of the court may request an answer to a petition for rehearing or rehearing en banc or a vote on such a petition.

MANDATE

The mandate is the document by which the court of appeals formally notifies the district court of its decision and by which jurisdiction for any necessary additional proceedings is conferred upon the district court. The mandate is issued by the clerk of court 21 days after judgment is entered unless a petition for rehearing has been filed or unless otherwise ordered by the court. If a petition for rehearing is filed, the mandate is issued seven days after denial of rehearing or, if a rehearing is granted, 21 days after the judgment is entered after rehearing. These times may be shortened or enlarged by court order. Fed. R. App. P. 41(a).

The losing party may request by motion that the issuance of the mandate be stayed in order to maintain the status quo during the pendency of an application for a writ of certiorari to the Supreme Court. The circuit court may require that a bond be posted as a condition to staying the issuance of the mandate.

MOTIONS

During the course of an appeal a variety of motions may be filed by the parties. Most of these are procedural and, to the extent permitted by the Federal Rules of Appellate Procedure, most courts have authorized their clerks of court to act upon motions if they are uncontested. Common procedural motions that may be acted on by the clerk of court are motions for:

1. Extensions of time to perform any of the acts required by local rules or the Federal Rules of Appellate Procedure;
2. Relief from specific requirements of the local rules or the Federal Rules of Appellate Procedure;
3. Permission to alter the form or content of the record on appeal;
4. Leave to file amicus curiae briefs;

5. Delay in the issuance of the mandate; and

6. Voluntary dismissal of the appeal.

Other motions, which require action by a judge or panel of judges, are those:

1. Relating to criminal cases or suits for post-conviction relief such as motions for:

   a. appointment of counsel;

   b. leave to appeal in forma pauperis;

   c. certificates of probable cause; and

   d. bail pending appeal;

2. For stays or injunctions pending appeal;

3. For leave to file interlocutory appeals;

4. Relating to stays granted in the district court;

5. For permission to file a brief containing more pages than the number fixed by the rules;

6. Relating to the time to be allowed for oral argument; and

7. To dismiss an appeal filed by the appellee.

In most courts the staff counsel's office is responsible for processing these motions and otherwise assisting the court in disposing of them.

EMERGENCY PROCEEDINGS

Both district courts and courts of appeals are frequently asked to make decisions on an emergency basis. In the appellate courts, these occasions usually arise when a litigant or a lower court is about to take some action that may irreparably injure another. The potentially aggrieved party seeks redress by motion for stay or injunction pending appeal or by petition for writ of mandamus or prohibition. In the district courts, these matters usually arise through a request for a temporary restraining order.

Each court has developed internal procedures for handling these matters efficiently, but the procedures differ so much that it is not possible to make a generalized description. The law clerk must become familiar with the procedures established by the local rules and the judge's own practices.

§ 5. Special Courts

The clerk may also encounter litigation from one of the various special courts established by Congress. The name "special courts" derives from their specialized jurisdiction.

COURT OF APPEALS FOR THE FEDERAL CIRCUIT

The most important special court is the Court of Appeals for the Federal Circuit, created in 1982 by merger of two existing courts, the U.S. Court of Customs and Patent Appeals and the appellate jurisdiction of the Court of Claims, the trial division of which is now the U.S. Claims Court. This court of appeals, which is based in Washington, has jurisdiction over appeals from: district courts in cases involving patents and certain claims against the U.S., the U.S. Claims Court, the Court of International Trade, the Court of Veterans Affairs, the Merit Systems Protection Board, the patent and trademark office, the boards that decide government contract issues, and a few other Article I agencies.

CLAIMS COURT

The U.S. Claims Court, an Article I trial court whose judges serve for 15-year terms, has jurisdiction of claims against the United States.

COURT OF INTERNATIONAL TRADE

The Court of International Trade, based in New York, hears cases concerning the value or classification of imports. The judges of this court are appointed under Article III and hold office during good behavior. Its judges may sit by designation on other Article III courts.

SPECIAL COURTS WITH REVOLVING MEMBERSHIP

Congress has created some courts whose judges do not sit permanently on those courts but are assigned to them in addition to their regular judicial assignment for terms of varying length. These include:

Judicial Panel on Multidistrict Litigation, created to consider transferring civil actions involving one or more common questions of fact pending in different districts to a single district for coordinated or consolidated pretrial proceedings. The panel consists of seven judges, district and circuit, appointed by the Chief Justice. The panel maintains a roster of "transferee judges" to whom it assigns the cases it certifies for transfer. (For discussion of multidistrict litigation problems, see p. 27).

Temporary Emergency Court of Appeals, created by Congress as part of the Economic Stabilization Act Amendments of 1971. The court has jurisdiction over appeals arising from that Act and regulations issued under it. Its judges are assigned by the Chief Justice from the roster of active and senior Article III judges. (At its March 1987 meeting, the Judicial Conference endorsed legislation to abolish this court.)

Railway Court, created by Congress as part of the Regional Rail Reorganization Act of 1973. This court resolves problems arising from the transfer of private railway property to the Conrail system. Its three judges are chosen by the Judicial Panel on Multidistrict Litigation. 45 U.S.C. § 718.

§ 6. Article I Courts

Congress has created many tribunals to assist it in meeting its legislative responsibilities under Article I of the Constitution. These courts do not exercise judicial power conferred by Article III, and their judges are appointed for fixed terms rather than during good behavior. They include the many administrative law judges serving in the executive agencies, who hear disputes over claims and benefits, subject to review by agency officials.

U.S. TAX COURT

The history of the Tax Court originates with the Revenue Act of 1924. The Act established the court as the U.S. Board of Tax Appeals in the executive branch of the government. In 1942 its name was changed to the Tax Court of the United States. As part of the Tax Reform Act of 1969, Congress reconstituted the Tax Court of the United States as the U.S. Tax Court.

The Tax Court has jurisdiction over controversies involving deficiencies determined by the Commissioner of Internal Revenue in income, estate, and gift taxes. The court also has jurisdiction to redetermine deficiencies in certain excise taxes and in windfall profits taxes; to redetermine liabilities of certain transferees and fiduciaries; to issue declaratory judgments related to the qualified status of retirement plans, the tax-exempt status of charitable organizations, and the status of certain governmental obligations; and to decide certain cases involving the disclosure of tax information by the Commissioner of Internal Revenue.

The Tax Court uses the Federal Rules of Evidence and its own rules of practice and procedure. The Tax Court's decisions are generally reviewable by the courts of appeals and by the Supreme Court. In cases in which the amount of tax in dispute does not exceed $10,000, simplified procedures are available at the option of the taxpayer. In these cases, however, the decision of the Tax Court is final and is not subject to review by any other court.

The Tax Court consists of 19 judges who are appointed by the President, with the advice and consent of the Senate, to serve for terms of 15 years. Its strength is augmented by Tax Court senior judges, who are recalled by the chief judge to perform further judicial duties, and by staff members who are designated special trial judges and are appointed by the chief judge.

The principal office of the Tax Court is located at 400 Second Street, N.W., Washington, D.C. 20217. The court maintains a field office in Los Angeles, California, and conducts trial sessions in more than 75 other cities throughout the United States.

CHAPTER 4. COURT MANAGEMENT

§ 1. Introduction

FEDERAL JUDICIAL ADMINISTRATION

Each of the 94 district and 13 federal circuit courts is responsible for its own management, subject, however, to statutory restrictions and policies set by national and regional judicial administrative agencies. The national agencies are the Judicial Conference of the United States and its agent, the Administrative Office of the U.S. Courts. The Federal Judicial Center has educational and research, but no administrative, responsibilities. To the degree possible, administrative policy-making is decentralized. Judicial councils in each regional circuit set administrative policy for the courts within the circuit with staff assistance by circuit executives, but most of the day-to-day administrative policy-making is the responsibility of the individual courts. Clerks of the district courts and, in some of the larger courts, district court executives provide staff assistance to those courts. Although law clerks will typically have limited direct relationships with most of these agencies (except the Administrative Office), a brief description of each will explain the national organizational framework within which the courts work.

CHIEF JUSTICE OF THE UNITED STATES

The Chief Justice is not only the presiding officer of the Supreme Court but also chairs the Judicial Conference of the United States and speaks for the federal judiciary in its administrative relations with the other branches of government and in its relations to the public at large. Congress has authorized the Chief Justice to employ an administrative assistant to help in discharging these responsibilities. The administrative assistant provides staff assistance and advice in all areas outside the decisional process.

JUDICIAL CONFERENCE OF THE UNITED STATES

The Chief Justice is presiding officer of the Judicial Conference of the United States, which is composed of the chief judge of each of the courts of appeals, one district judge elected by the district and circuit judges in each of the regional circuits, and the chief judge of the Court of International Trade. Its forerunner was created in 1922 at the urging of Chief Justice Taft to provide the federal courts with some degree of coordination in developing policy recommendations and to transfer judges temporarily to assist in easing backlogs.

The Conference usually meets twice a year and is served by an extensive system of committees, including an Executive Committee. Conference business includes budgetary matters, administrative questions, legislative recommendations, and proposed changes in the federal rules of procedure and evidence. (These proposed changes become law if approved by the Conference, the Supreme Court, and the Congress.)

ADMINISTRATIVE OFFICE OF THE U.S. COURTS

The Administrative Office, whose director and deputy director are appointed by the Supreme Court, is the "housekeeping" agency of the federal courts and is the operational arm of the Judicial Conference. Under general Judicial Conference guidance, it is responsible for all matters of federal judicial administration that are thought to need national coordination or direction. These range from setting salary and staffing levels in the courts to collecting workload statistics and administering the federal courts' budget. The *Annual Report of the Director* of the Administrative Office, published along with the proceedings of the Judicial Conference, provides detailed statistical data on all phases of federal court operations.

The Administrative Office Telephone Directory lists the various offices and units of the Administrative Office.

CIRCUIT JUDICIAL COUNCILS

Circuit judicial councils were created in 1939 by the same statute that created the Administrative Office. The chief judge of the circuit is the presiding officer of each circuit council. The council includes a specific number of circuit judges and district judges determined separately in each circuit according to 28 U.S.C. § 332(a)(1)(B). If, by majority vote of the active circuit judges, there are fewer than six circuit judges on the council, the council must include at least two district judges. If there are six or more circuit judges on the council, the council must include at least three district judges. Creation of the councils reflected a commitment to decentralized administration. The councils must review numerous district court operational plans (for jury utilization and defense of indigents, for example), monitor pending caseload statistics in the courts, and take action as appropriate. They also review complaints of judicial misconduct that the chief circuit judge has not resolved or dismissed as unmeritorious. The circuit council does not have responsibility for preparing local rules for the district courts, or bankruptcy courts, but Fed. R. Civ. P. 83 and Fed. R. Crim. P. 57 imply that the counsel is obliged to review all local rules to be certain they do not conflict with the national rules. Councils are authorized to appoint a circuit executive to provide them administrative assistance (see p. 121).

The circuit court of appeals meets separately from the council, prescribes the local rules of the circuit court, and administers the business of that court.

CIRCUIT JUDICIAL CONFERENCES

The district, circuit, and bankruptcy judges of each circuit are required by statute to attend an annual conference to consider ways of improving the administration of justice in the circuit. The statute, 28 U.S.C. § 333, mandates participation by the bar in such conferences. The format of these conferences varies considerably from circuit to circuit, but they usually feature educational programs of different types, devoted to developments in the law and legal procedure.

FEDERAL JUDICIAL CENTER

Congress created the Federal Judicial Center in 1967 as the courts' research and education agency. 28 U.S.C. § 620. Its policies are set by a Board that includes the Chief Justice, as chairman, the Director of the Administrative Office, and six other judges elected by the Judicial Conference. It is responsible for designing and sponsoring programs for continuing education and training of judges and other court personnel, policy research on matters of judicial administration, and developing technological applications for court and case management. The organization of the Center is explained in its *Annual Report* and outlined in the Administrative Office Telephone Directory.

RESOURCE ALLOCATION

The annual budget for the operation of the federal courts, exclusive of the Supreme Court, has been over $1 billion since 1985. This is considerably less than 1 percent of the total federal budget. Salaries of judges and supporting personnel represent the largest component of the federal judicial budget. Other major cost items are space and facilities, operational and maintenance expenses, juror fees and related costs, and expenses for services of public defenders.

The judiciary budget is administered by the Administrative Office under the supervision of the Judicial Conference.

CHIEF JUDGES

Each court of appeals and each district court has a chief judge, as do bankruptcy courts with more than one judge.

Chief judges have no authority over the actual decision of cases by other judges. In judicial matters, their authority is exactly the same as that of any other judge.

A vacancy in the chief judgeship of an Article III court is filled by the active judge who, at the time of the vacancy, is senior in commission, under 65 years of age, has served on the court at least a year, and has not previously served as chief judge. No judge may serve as chief judge beyond the age of 70 unless no younger judge is eligible to become chief judge or acting chief judge. Upon request, a chief judge may be relieved of the duties of that office and remain an active judge (see "Active and Senior Judges," p. 84). In that event, the active judge of the court next most senior in commission who meets the criteria and is willing to serve is designated by the Chief Justice as the chief judge. In bankruptcy courts with more than one judge, the district judges, by majority vote, designate one of the bankruptcy judges as chief judge. The chief district judge makes the designation if a majority of the district judges cannot agree.

Chief Judges—Courts of Appeals

The chief judge of a circuit supervises its staff and handles most of the administrative details for the court of appeals. In addition, the chief judge presides at judicial council meetings and judicial conferences in their circuits; serves as one of the circuit's representatives to the Judicial Conference of the United States; assigns the circuit judges of their circuits to temporary duty on district courts within the circuit; assigns district judges in the circuit to other courts; appoints members of three-judge courts when such appointments are necessary; certifies to the Chief Justice the need for temporary assistance from additional judges from other circuits; and supervises the circuit executive. In most circuits, the chief judge appoints committees of judges or individual judges to assist in various administrative matters, such as the composition of panels and the scheduling of sittings. The court usually has regular meetings to discuss administrative matters.

Chief Judges—District Courts

The chief judges of district courts take much of the responsibility for the administration of the court. Usually, they supervise the clerk's office, the probation office, the pretrial services office if there is one, and the magistrates, and have oversight responsibility for the bankruptcy court. By statute the chief judge is responsible for carrying out the rules and orders of the court that divide the court's business among the judges, 28 U.S.C. § 137, and for appointing magistrates when a majority of the judges in the district do not concur, 28 U.S.C. § 631. In some district courts, the chief judge appoints committees of judges or individual judges to assist in various administrative matters. In some district courts, the judges meet regularly; in others, they consult each other only as the need arises. In most courts the allotment of cases to judges is made by the clerk of court according to a random procedure, but the chief judge may on occasion make a special assignment for an unusual case, such as one of considerable length or complexity.

Chief Judges—Bankruptcy Courts

The chief bankruptcy judges' statutory duties, like those of chief circuit and district judges, are phrased generally. The chief judge is to "ensure that the rules of the bankruptcy court and of the district court are observed and that the business of the bankruptcy court is handled effectively and expeditiously." 28 U.S.C. § 154(b). The office of chief bankruptcy judge is new and its duties presumably will evolve as have the duties of the other chief judges.

ACTIVE AND SENIOR JUDGES

An Article III judge who attains the age of 65 may elect to become a senior judge if that judge has 15 years of service or the "rule of 80" applies (that is, if the judge's age and years of service combined total 80). This action is entirely at the option of the judge, who may continue to be an active judge indefinitely. If a judge elects senior status, a vacancy is created, which is filled in the usual manner by presidential appointment and senatorial confirmation. Judges on senior status have retired "from regular active service," 28 U.S.C. § 371(b), but they continue to receive the salary of an active judge on the same court. Senior judges who perform substantial judicial service are entitled, upon certification of the judicial council, to an office staff equivalent to that of active judges or to such lesser number of assistants as their work may require.

Some circuits have adopted guidelines for these staff requirements. Senior judges often continue to serve their courts, usually taking a reduced caseload and requesting that they not be assigned to certain types of routine cases. Some senior district judges, for example, request that Social Security appeals or criminal cases not be assigned to them. Senior judges on appellate courts usually participate only in oral argument cases and not in deciding motions or cases disposed of without oral argument. Particularly in recent years, with the increasing caseloads experienced in the federal judicial system, the services rendered by senior judges have become vital to the operation of the courts.

The Chief Justice may assign judges to serve temporarily in other circuits. Senior judges are sometimes especially appropriate choices for such assignments. The assignments may include protracted cases requiring an extended period of temporary service.

Judges who meet the "rule of 80" may also "retire from the office," in which case they are no longer judicial officers. They may not continue to hear cases, but they are entitled to an annuity equal to their salary at the time of retirement. 28 U.S.C. § 371(a). Of course, judges who do not meet the requirement of the "rule of 80" may simply resign from office.

§ 2. Office Administration

Effective office management is essential to the prompt and efficient administration of justice. Efficient procedures make it possible for the court to complete assigned work sooner; to manage the trial judge's trial, motion, and conference schedules; to manage case handling in the circuit judge's office; to determine what records must be kept and preserved and what records are duplicative or unnecessary; and to assure that sufficient time has been reserved for the court to fulfill essential judicial duties, including, for example, trials, court sittings, and the drafting of opinions and orders.

KEYS

A clerk should obtain a key to the judge's office and a key to the library, if there is a separate library. Ordinarily a clerk will not need a key to the building because most federal courthouse buildings have one entrance that is open at all hours. A clerk may gain entrance to the building after hours or on weekends by entering through that door and signing the register. The guards usually come to know the law clerks within a short while but may still ask them to present identification. Some building managers prepare building passes to assist clerks in identifying themselves when entering at other than normal business hours.

TELEPHONE USAGE AND MESSAGES

1. The telephone should be answered promptly, and basic rules of politeness and etiquette apply.

2. Some judges instruct that the office telephone be attended during all working hours, including lunch periods. Many have installed an automatic answering unit on which callers may leave a message for use during lunch hours or when all members of the judge's staff are in the courtroom.

3. When receiving calls, identify the office (e.g., "Judge Smith's chambers").

4. If the judge is not available to receive a call, offer to take the name, number, and message of the caller to enable the judge to return the call. Be certain to get the number and spelling of the name correctly, reading it back if necessary.

    Some lawyers hesitate to ask that a judge return their calls, but some judges prefer to do so and the caller should be so informed. Other judges prefer to receive a detailed message so that a return call can be avoided; if so, callers should be encouraged to describe the reason for their call.

5. If the call relates to a case, the message should contain the name and number of the case. In addition, it should contain a description of the problem to which the call relates.

6. Though each judge may have an individual preference for telephone etiquette, some prefer that callers not be screened because screening creates the impression that the judge will not talk to "ordinary" people. A caller should be asked to give the caller's name when the judge is awaiting a call from a particular person and will speak only to that person (e.g., because the judge is in conference) or is out of the office and has left a message for a particular person.

7. Do not keep a caller waiting on the line. If a lawyer is put on "hold" while the clerk determines the answer to the question, or while the lawyer waits to speak to the judge, someone should check back periodically to ask if the caller wants to continue holding, and to indicate that the caller has not been forgotten.

8. Most judges prefer not to be interrupted when in conference. Some judges also request that their calls be held at other times to allow them an uninterrupted period for concentrated activity. If the judge is not available, it is appropriate to say "The judge is in trial," or "The judge is in conference," or "The judge is out of the office," but some judges prefer that the reason for the judge's unavailability not be communicated to the caller.

9. If the judge is not in the office, the appropriate response is, "The judge is not in the office at this time; may I take a message?" Some statements may convey a bad impression and should therefore be avoided (e.g., "The judge has said to hold all calls," "The judge can't be disturbed," or "The judge hasn't come in yet.").

10. Important phone calls may require documentation through correspondence or an office memorandum, and sometimes through a minute entry.

FTS Telephone System

Official long-distance calls are to be made only on the FTS (Federal Telecommunications System) telephone system, unless the judge specifically directs otherwise. The FTS consists of direct lines operated by the General Services Administration connected with the chambers of most federal judges, other government offices, and long-distance lines operated by access through the FTS. The judge's secretary will usually have an FTS directory with instructions for use. Long-distance calls by ordinary means result in additional billing by the telephone company directly to the judge's number. Such calls should not be placed unless the judge specifically directs. Directory service is available only at an additional charge and should be used only when published telephone books do not contain the needed number.

The FTS system is for official calls only. Government telephones should not be used for personal calls except as specifically provided by regulations. Federal Information Resources Management Regulations stipulate:

> The use of Government telephone systems (including calls over commercial systems which will be paid for by the Government) shall be limited to the conduct of official business. Official business calls include emergency calls and calls that are considered to be in the best interest of the Government. A call may be considered as properly authorized as being in the best interest of the Government if it satisfies the following criteria:
>
> (1) It does not adversely affect the performance of official duties by the employee or the employee's organization.
>
> (2) It is of reasonable duration and frequency.
>
> (3) It reasonably could not be made at another time.

CORRESPONDENCE AND OTHER MAIL

Most judges do not open the mail but instruct a secretary or law clerk to do so except for those envelopes marked "Personal" or "Confidential."

Because federal judges are occasionally the targets of terrorists, caution should be exercised when the mail is opened. Common recognition points for letter and package bombs include:

- foreign mail, air mail, and special delivery;
- restrictive markings, such as confidential, personal, etc.;
- excessive postage;
- handwritten or poorly typed addresses;
- incorrect titles;
- titles but no names;
- misspellings of common words;
- oily stains or discolorations;
- no return address;

- rigid envelope;
- lopsided or uneven envelope;
- protruding wires or tinfoil;
- excessive securing material such as masking tape, string, etc.
- drawings, diagrams, or illustrations.

If a letter or package arouses the attention of the person responsible for opening the mail, either the secretary or clerk, that person should notify the marshal's office or court security officer immediately.

The incoming mail should be reviewed early in the day because it may relate to matters scheduled for that day. Some mail will be library materials, such as new pocket parts. Most judges will want to have specified advance sheets and other materials describing current decisions or legislation put on their desks for review before the materials are shelved in the library.

Depending upon office procedure, either the judge, a secretary, or a clerk will first review the correspondence and make an initial decision concerning how it should be handled. Some will be correspondence from non-lawyers, which is dealt with in the next section. Other correspondence will relate to cases pending before the court. Some correspondence will contain awaited memoranda of law on pending motions or trials. Some will ask for rescheduling or continuance of motion hearings or trials, though some judges require that such requests be made by formal motion. In the court of appeals, much of the correspondence will be from other judges and from the clerk's office.

In all courts, correspondence that requires a response should be answered on the day it is received, if possible. In the trial courts, the judge may direct a clerk to telephone all counsel with a verbal response or to draft a letter to all counsel in response. When correspondence referring to a pending suit is forwarded to any counsel of record over the signature of the judge or law clerk, copies should be sent to *all* other counsel of record, showing at the bottom of the letter (with the identifying abbreviation "cc") the names of the other persons who are receiving copies. The issuance of identical communications to all parties signals that no ex parte communication has occurred and avoids consequent criticism of such undesirable judicial action. Letters requiring more complex responses, for example, a new date for the hearing of a motion, may require the judge's review.

Correspondence from an appellate judge will seldom be sent directly to counsel but to the clerk of court with instructions concerning how the clerk of court should reply, for the appellate judge writes for a panel or the court rather than individually.

Chapter 5 contains suggestions on the drafting of correspondence.

CORRESPONDENCE FROM NON-LAWYERS

Correspondence from non-lawyers is important because the public's opinions about the fairness, responsiveness, and effectiveness of the judiciary are affected by the promptness and appropriateness of the court's answers.

In the district court, some of the correspondence from the public relates to requests to be excused from jury duty. That subject is dealt with under "Case Management: The Trial Court," p. 95. Some correspondence contains character references on behalf of a person who has been convicted of a crime and who is scheduled for sentencing. Judges differ in their manner of handling such correspondence. Most simply acknowledge receiving the letter and refer it to the probation office.

Other correspondence may express a reaction to a ruling of the court. Whether positive or negative, expressions of opinion by members of the public generally call only for courteous acknowledgment, not for an explanation or justification of the court's action. If a letter requests information about a ruling, most judges simply acknowledge receipt of the letter and send a copy of the opinion. If more information is requested, most judges refer the writer to the record. See Chapter 2 for comments regarding the relationship between law clerks and the media.

Some judges may wish to respond to a letter that indicates a misunderstanding concerning a significant fact, proceeding, or legal conclusion. Judges who adopt this policy may ask their law clerks to prepare a draft of a response for the judge to review. The response should not be argumentative or defensive; it should merely state the relevant facts or legal conclusion.

See p. 154 for a discussion of correspondence from prisoners.

THE OPENING OF COURT

In most appellate courts, law clerks do not have the responsibility for opening court. In district courts, they frequently do. Find out from the courtroom deputy what method the judge uses and follow that procedure. One method, for example, is for the law clerk to rap on the door before the judge enters, open the door, then call out: "All rise." The judge then enters and walks to the bench. The clerk walks to the front of the bench and says: "Oyez! Oyez! Oyez! The Honorable United States District Court for the Eastern District of Louisiana is now in session." (In some courts the crier adds: "Judge Smith presiding. All those having business before the court please come forward and be heard.") "God save the United States and this Honorable Court." The judge usually stands during this call, then says, "Please be seated," and sits down.

MAINTAINING THE LIBRARY

Each day's mail will bring something for the library: advance sheets, pocket parts, slip opinions, replacement volumes, and inserts for loose-leaf services. Filing these in the appropriate locations is usually the clerk's responsibility. If they are put away daily, the chore of maintaining the library will not be burdensome; if they are left to accumulate, not only is the job more demanding but in addition the library is incomplete and unreliable.

Every book received must be stamped promptly with a rubber stamp that identifies it as property of the United States. The clerk should keep track of books borrowed by attorneys for courtroom use. The clerk should never allow books to be taken outside the chambers and courtroom.

The clerk should promptly reshelve books used during the course of research. They will then be easier to find, and the library will be neater. The clerk should also be sure that legal pads, book markers, pencils, and ballpoint pens are always available in the library.

Generally, advertisements in the various legal periodicals will keep the clerk abreast of new publications. The clerk should not hesitate to suggest additions to the library.

MAINTENANCE OF OFFICE RECORDS

A clerk may be assigned responsibility for maintaining some of the records in the judge's office including:

1. Case files;
2. Trial schedules or calendars;
3. "Tickler" records to remind about future case activities;
4. Indices to the judge's prior decisions;
5. Indices to slip opinions; and
6. Work papers relating to cases in progress. (If the clerk is given this job, the clerk should learn when and how entries should be made.)

The clerk may also find it helpful to make a collection of materials used frequently in the judge's office if earlier clerks have not done so. This may include forms, office procedure checklists, and samples of work product. These will be useful references and, if kept current, will be invaluable to successor clerks.

If case records are being used in the judge's chambers it is the clerk's responsibility to be certain that they are not misplaced and that they are returned to the office of the clerk of court as soon as the judge and the clerk have finished with them.

OFFICE FORM BOOK

Because most law clerks serve only a year or two, an office form book is helpful to educate new clerks and to provide continuity and consistency in office administration. The form book may contain samples of letters, orders, opinions, jury charges, minute entries, and office or file memoranda written by prior clerks. The form book describes the format and method of presentation of written documents issued by the court or presented to the judge by the clerk. If the judge has such a book, the clerk should use it. If not, the clerk may wish to ask whether the judge would like to have one compiled.

PREPARING FOR OUT-OF-TOWN TRIPS

Many courts sit in more than one location and many judges require their clerks to attend out-of-town sessions of court. Arrangements for court trips may sometimes be the clerk's responsibility. Even if the judge's secretary or the office of the clerk of court organizes the judge's travel, each clerk will have to make personal arrangements. The following checklist will be helpful:

1. If commercial transportation is to be used, make reservations as early as possible. Tickets are usually purchased with Government Travel Requests rather than with cash.

2. Make necessary hotel or motel reservations (many hotels and motels give discounts to government employees).

3. If necessary, apply to the clerk of court for an advance payment toward travel expenses on the official form used for that purpose.

4. Take along:

   a. necessary case files and materials;

   b. any personal notes or memoranda relating to the cases to be heard;

   c. the judge's robe;

   d. paper, pencils, stationery, and other needed supplies (if the site for the out-of-town session is one that is frequently used by the court, there may be a permanent stock of stationery and supplies);

   e. necessary equipment such as a gavel, and recording or dictating equipment;

   f. the briefs and any other case materials; and

   g. mailing labels and envelopes for returning any items that the judge and the clerks may not wish to carry back.

PER DIEM EXPENSES FOR TRAVEL

A clerk accompanying a judge during travel out of town on court business will be reimbursed for expenses of food and lodging and related expenses, according to the detailed rules set forth in vol. I, ch. V, *Guide to Judiciary Policies and Procedures*. These rules generally reimburse either (a) a flat dollar amount per day regardless of actual expenses or (b) itemized actual expenses, but not in excess of a fixed dollar amount. An advance of expense money can be obtained by completing a form and taking it to the office of the clerk of court. This advance must be listed on the travel voucher filed after completing the trip. The judge's secretary can supply these forms.

§ 3. Local Rules of Court

Fed. R. Civ. P. 83 and Fed. R. Crim. P. 57 authorize district courts to adopt local rules. B.R. 9029 provides similar authority to bankruptcy courts. Local rules must be consistent with the national rules and may be abrogated by the circuit judicial council. 28 U.S.C. § 2077 directs the courts of appeal to publish their procedural rules, including internal operating procedures.

These local rules include the procedure for setting cases for trial, scheduling pretrial conferences, setting motions for oral argument, serving memoranda of law, and other details relating to trial. They may also state the procedure for admission of attorneys to practice in the specific district or circuit, the term of the court, the functions of the clerk of court, rules regarding the filing of motions, and more specific data such as the number of copies required to be filed, limitations on the length of memoranda, the time within which memoranda must be filed, and restrictions on page length, typeface, and margin size. The Information Services of the Federal Judicial Center maintains a collection of all district court local rules but the courts themselves are the best sources for up-to-date versions of their rules.

Each circuit court has local rules concerning procedures for ordering transcripts, filing and docketing the appeal, calendaring, motions, summary disposition of appeals, setting cases for oral argument, time limitations on oral argument, petitions for rehearing, petitions for en banc consideration, and stay of mandate. The local rules and internal operating procedures (IOPs) of the circuits are printed in the *United States Code Annotated* following title 28, the Judicial Code.

A copy of the local rules of court and of the court's internal operating procedures is the law clerk's basic handbook on procedure in the clerk's own district or circuit. A pamphlet copy of the district or circuit rules and internal operating procedures may be obtained at the office of the clerk of court. Immediately upon beginning work a clerk should obtain a copy of each of these, carefully read them, and keep the copies for ready reference.

Local rules are often revised by an order of the court. The clerk should be certain to obtain all loose sheets and other later addenda that have been adopted after the pamphlet was published.

§ 4. Case Management: The Trial Court

The responsibility for moving a case through the trial court is not solely that of the attorneys, and the function of the court is not simply to be available if and when counsel want a hearing. With the caseload increasing each year and even those cases requiring prompt decision forced to wait for judicial attention, the disposition of all cases as speedily as is consistent with justice has become of paramount importance. Private counsel may have many personal reasons either to expedite or to delay a trial: other more insistent clients, relative fees to be earned, procrastination, or lack of familiarity with procedures, to name but a few. Litigants whose cases are not promptly tried may conclude that the fault lies entirely with the courts. The Federal Rules of Civil Procedure are to be "construed to secure the just, speedy, and inexpensive determination of every action," Fed. R. Civ. P. 1, and many judges consider this not only as an instruction for interpreting the rules but as a mandate to the judge to seek these goals. These judges believe that it is the duty of the courts to protect the public interest by participating actively and insistently in the process of moving cases from filing to determination. Effective docket control means that early in the life of a case the court should assume responsibility for guiding it to a final conclusion. A preliminary conference should be held, and dates for steps in the case fixed. This may include establishing deadlines for filing motions, a time limit for discovery, a date for counsel to take the next step in its prosecution, and preferably a trial date.

OFFICE STATUS SHEETS

Some judges maintain an office status sheet on a bulletin board in the chambers library, or in some other convenient location. Its purpose is to keep the judge and the clerks advised of legal matters under advisement and awaiting disposition. When a matter has been taken under advisement, the clerk assigned to the case should write it on the status sheet as soon as the assignment is made to prevent its being overlooked.

It is also a good practice for each clerk to keep a personal status sheet, which can be revised each week. This sheet should list all of the matters for which the clerk has responsibility. Using it will enable the clerk to make effective use of the available time and remember all pending assignments.

Some judges require their secretaries to keep in their word processors an inventory of all pending matters, the initials or name of the clerk assigned to work on the matter, and any other pertinent information. If such a list is maintained, the clerk should be sure to keep the secretary advised of all matters assigned, matters completed, and other relevant status information.

Many judges are now using computers for docket control, to maintain case inventories and case-status records. While this is the most effective and comprehensive method, any other system may be employed so long as it is regularly maintained and continually monitored.

CALENDARING SYSTEMS

In multi-judge trial courts it is necessary to have a system for determining which judge has the responsibility for each case. These systems fall into three general categories: the individual calendar, the master calendar, and a system that combines features of the other two.

In an individual calendar system each case is assigned to a particular judge at the time it is filed or soon thereafter and that judge then has complete responsibility for that case until it is terminated. All federal district courts now use this system and have established random case-assignment systems to ensure equalization of the workload among the judges and to prevent the litigants from being able to anticipate or influence the selection of the judge to whom their case is assigned. There are also standard procedures for reassigning cases in which the original judge is disqualified, for assuring that related cases are all assigned to the same judge, and for special assignment of unusual and protracted cases. These are all described in the local rules.

In the master calendar system, which was once used in the federal courts and is still used in many state courts, each judge has equal responsibility for all pending cases in the court. The cases are pooled. All motions in a given calendar period are assigned to one or more judges, as the volume of work requires. Other judges are assigned to trials, and, on any given court day, cases that are ready for trial are distributed, usually by an assignment judge, to the other sitting judges. The adherents of this system suggest that it makes the most efficient use of judge time, while its critics assert that it prevents fixing responsibility for decision and encourages litigants to make repetitious contentions. Moreover, each time a ruling is required a new judge must become familiar with the law and facts of the case.

Some courts using the individual calendar system periodically set trials on a master calendar to expedite the trial process.

TRIAL SCHEDULING AND TRIAL PREPARATION

A single trial may be set for a specific date or the court may set multiple cases for trial on the same day. Some courts use the "trailing calendar" or "trailing docket," in which the court schedules a number of cases for trial beginning on a stated date. The cases are tried in the order reflected by the schedule. Counsel themselves have the responsibility for obtaining information from the court and the attorneys whose cases precede them on the calendar about the progress of those cases so that they may be ready to go to trial whenever the court reaches their case.

More than 90 percent of all civil cases filed are disposed of by rulings on motions, or settled before trial. If only an additional 10 percent of all cases filed went to trial, the court's trial volume would be doubled. Many judges and commentators believe that the highest quality of justice results from a freely negotiated settlement arrived at between equally skilled and equally informed and prepared advocates. Settlement achieves a solution to a controversy earlier and at less cost than a trial. When the case involves only the interests of the parties, negotiated settlement may therefore be desirable. If the case involves an issue of public importance, however, adjudication may be the method of disposition that better meets the needs of justice. Some judges therefore may not press for settlement of such cases. Whatever settlement negotiations may occur, however, the lawyers should be thoroughly prepared to try a case when it is reached. Some courts issue specific written instructions to attorneys stating their responsibilities for trial preparation.

If settlement is to be reached, negotiations should be timely completed. When a settlement takes place a few hours or even a day before a scheduled trial, the court's schedule may be disrupted, leaving the judges, and sometimes jurors, with unscheduled time. Counsel have spent time preparing for trial, witnesses have been subpoenaed, and the expenses of litigation increased. The trailing calendar and other multiple-case-setting devices are intended to alleviate problems caused by last-minute settlement by providing substitute cases to replace those that do not go to trial. This relieves the court's problems but does not reduce the problems caused to litigants and counsel by eve-of-trial settlements.

JURY MANAGEMENT

Random Juror Selection

The selection of grand and petit jurors is governed by 28 U.S.C. §§ 1861–1874. Each district has a jury selection plan that has been approved by the circuit judicial council and the chief judge or the chief judge's designee.

The goal of the selection process is to assure "grand and petit juries selected at random from a fair cross section of the community in the district or division wherein the court convenes," 28 U.S.C. § 1861, and to avoid excluding any citizen "from service as a grand or petit juror . . . on account of race, color, religion, sex, national origin or economic status," 28 U.S.C. § 1862.

The process of selecting prospective jurors is managed by the clerk of the court or, in a few courts, by a jury commission consisting of one citizen resident within the district and the clerk, as determined in each court's jury selection plan. The process is carried out under the supervision and control of the court.

Because of the different situation in each district, each jury selection process is somewhat different, but the process is generally as follows:

1. A random selection of prospective jurors' names is made by computer or manually, using voter registration lists or other sources specified by the court's plan. The names thus selected are placed in a master jury wheel. The minimum number of names in the master jury wheel must be one-half of 1 percent of the number on the source lists or 1,000, whichever is less;

2. As needed by the court, names are drawn publicly at random from the master jury wheel, and jury-qualification questionnaires are sent to those persons whose names are drawn;

3. From the responses to the questionnaires a determination is made as to which persons are qualified for jury service and which persons are disqualified, exempt, or excused;

4. The names of those who have been determined to be qualified are placed in a second jury wheel consisting of qualified jurors;

5. As needed, names are selected from the qualified jury wheel, and lists of the names selected are prepared; and

6. Summonses are issued to the necessary number of persons needed for the jury venire several weeks in advance of each trial calendar advising each of the time and place to report for jury service.

Exemptions, Disqualifications, and Excuses

A person is deemed qualified for jury service unless the person is:

1. Not a citizen of the United States;

2. Unable to read, write, and understand English with a degree of proficiency sufficient to fill out satisfactorily the jury qualification form;

3. Incapable of rendering satisfactory service because of mental or physical infirmity; or

4. Charged with (or has been convicted in a state or federal court of record of) a crime punishable by imprisonment for more than one year without subsequent restoration of civil rights. 28 U.S.C. § 1865.

Some district courts have adopted other specific exemptions.

These grounds for exemption from jury service are based on public interest and are specified in the court's jury-selection plan. 18 U.S.C. § 1863 requires the plan to provide for the exemption of members of the armed forces in active service; members of the fire or police departments of any state; and public officers of the federal, state, and local governments who are actively engaged in the performance of official duties.

Jury service is a citizen duty as well as a privilege, and excuses are not readily granted. A person may, however, be excused from jury service temporarily if the court finds that such service would result in undue hardship or extreme inconvenience. In such a case, the name of an excused juror is placed back in the qualified jury wheel. If approached about an excuse, the clerk should not indicate any attitude on the request but should simply agree to transmit it to the judge for action or inform the individual of the judge's procedure for action on such requests.

The court and all its staff should make every effort to see that those called for jury selection are treated with courtesy.

In multiple-judge courthouses it is common for several judges to begin jury trials at different hours to obtain maximum usage of the jurors summoned for jury duty, sending persons examined for jury duty and not selected to another courtroom so they can be examined for selection on another jury, and sometimes using jurors who have served in one trial in the next succeeding trial.

When prospective jury panels report for possible selection in a case, they should be segregated from other people in the courtroom. A portion of the spectator section should be cleared for their exclusive use.

Juror Orientation

Most courts conduct an orientation program for new jurors to inform them of their responsibilities and to explain the trial process in which they may participate. The Judicial Conference recommends two orientation films, one for grand jurors, the other for petit jurors.[*]

Voir Dire

The voir dire examination of jurors is conducted in most courts by the judge. Fed. R. Civ. P. 47 and Fed. R. Crim. P. 24, however, authorize the judge to permit the lawyers to do so. If the judge conducts the voir dire, the rules authorize counsel to submit specific voir dire questions that they want the judge to ask or areas of inquiry about which they want the jury examined, and the rules direct the judge to consider whether to ask them. Some judges permit counsel to conduct all or a part of the voir dire examination. In a few courts voir dire for civil juries (and sometimes for criminal juries) is conducted by or before the clerk or a magistrate rather than the judge, leaving the judge free to work on other matters until called upon to resolve any problems that arise during the examination of the jurors, but in some circuits neither magistrates nor clerks may be used to conduct voir dire in the Fifth Circuit. U.S. v. Ford, 824 F.2d 1430 (5th Cir. 1987) (en banc), *cert. denied,* 108 S. Ct. 741 (1988); U.S. v. Garcia, 848 F.2d 1324 (2d Cir. 1988).

Trial jurors are usually free to go where they wish during trial recesses and to go home at night. Occasionally, however, when there is unusual publicity about the trial or reason to believe that someone will attempt to exert improper influence on the jury, the court may direct that the jury be sequestered. When this occurs, the jury is kept together at all times and is supervised by deputy marshals when court is not in session. Jurors in criminal cases are usually sequestered from the time they begin deliberating until

---

[*] *And Justice for All* (1970) and *The Federal Grand Jury: The People's Panel* (1985) are probably available from the clerk of court. Information on purchasing copies is in the Federal Judicial Center's *Catalog of Audiovisual Media Programs.*

they reach a verdict. In civil cases, the judge may also sequester the jury from the time it begins deliberations until it reaches a verdict.

Jury Supervision

In most courts a deputy marshal is responsible for jury supervision. However, this responsibility may be assigned to a clerk. When assigned this responsibility, the clerk should be present in the chambers early enough in the morning to accommodate those members of the jury who arrive earlier than the normal court time. The jury room should be open and available for the use of the jurors as they arrive for work.

If it is the judge's policy to permit the jury to take notes, either the deputy clerk of court or the law clerk should, before the trial begins, place pads and pencils in numbered manila envelopes for distribution to the individual jurors. Extra pads, pencils, and envelopes should also be placed in the jury room for use during deliberations.

If the clerk is responsible for jury supervision, the clerk must ensure that there is no improper communication between jurors and litigants, lawyers, witnesses, or others attending court— whether in the courtroom, jury room, or in the hallways adjacent to the courtroom and chambers.

The clerk may also be required to be steward of the jury during deliberations. Some courts require the clerk to take a special oath with respect to this duty just before the jury retires. Once the oath is taken, the clerk assumes primary responsibility for guarding the jury until relieved of this duty by the judge. The clerk must remain outside the jury-room door during the entire deliberation process and must take every reasonable precaution to ensure that the jurors do not come into contact with other people, especially the litigants, their attorneys, or any witnesses. The clerk must *never* comment on the evidence, the litigants, the attorneys, or the witnesses to any juror (or, for that matter, to anyone else). If a juror has any question about the trial, at any stage, the clerk should simply state that such questions should be addressed to the court in writing. The clerk must not answer the question, however simple it may appear to be.

Juries are sometimes sent to lunch at government expense when deliberations are not completed before regular meal times. Occasionally, a jury will be sent to dinner if there is need for evening deliberations. In these situations, jurors will be accompanied by court personnel in order to prevent improper contact between the panel and outsiders. A catered meal may be ordered, to be eaten in the jury room, or the clerk, along with a deputy marshal, may accompany the jury to a local dining room, where tables must be provided for the jurors separate from all other diners. The clerk may be required to make appropriate reservations. The marshal is responsible for signing the bill for the meals and for keeping it within the budgetary limits set by the government. Jurors should be instructed not to drink alcoholic beverages.

DISTRIBUTING OPINIONS

Fed. R. Civ. P. 52(a) requires the judge to make findings of fact and conclusions of law in all actions tried on the facts without a jury or with an advisory jury. The rule permits the judge to do this orally or in writing, or, instead, to render an opinion or memorandum of decision. The district judge may also wish to write a formal opinion to explain rulings on particular motions. The judge's secretary sends the original of the findings or opinion and of any judgment to the docket clerk for filing in the official record. Then the secretary or clerk of court sends a copy of each set of findings or the opinion to each counsel of record, making and distributing other copies in accordance with the judge's instructions. In most district courts, the clerk of court handles the distribution of opinions, but in a few district courts, this responsibility falls to the law clerk.

The judge decides whether or not the opinion or findings are to be published. This connotes not only inclusion in a traditional case reporter, but also inclusion in on-line computer services, such as West Publishing Co.'s WESTLAW and Mead Data Central's LEXIS and in specialized reporting services. The publication procedure in district courts is not uniform. Some opinions may be sent only to West Publishing Co. and Mead Data; others (of unusual importance) may be sent to the Bureau of National Affairs; some may be sent to specialized publishers, such as American Maritime

Cases. Unless someone else is given this task, the clerk should check with the judge to determine whether the judge wishes the opinion to be published. If so, the clerk should make such distribution as the judge directs. In each case, the opinion should be accompanied by a cover letter from the judge. The judge may have a form letter for this purpose.

§ 5. Bankruptcy Courts

The organization of the bankruptcy courts is discussed at p. 43.

SPECIAL DUTIES OF CLERKS TO BANKRUPTCY JUDGES

The duties of a clerk to a bankruptcy judge are those of a clerk to a federal judge generally and those of a clerk to a trial judge specifically. The comments in this handbook regarding the difference between the duties of trial court clerks and those of appellate court clerks are applicable. The preferences of the judge are likely to have more influence on the functions performed by a bankruptcy judge's clerk than any inherent difference between a district court and a bankruptcy court. Of course, the subject matter of bankruptcy courts is limited to civil proceedings and most trials are bench trials. Because the bankruptcy judge is allowed only one clerk, the clerk to a bankruptcy judge can expect to have sole responsibility for assisting the judge.

The volume of cases and proceedings in bankruptcy court is generally greater than in other trial courts, resulting in a need for the clerk to exercise substantial organizational skills and efficient work habits. Trials and hearings in bankruptcy court differ from those in district court principally in that bankruptcy hearings are more numerous and more expedited. For the clerk that means more scheduling problems, more substantial prehearing preparation of memoranda, and shorter time limits. It also means more pressure for the clerk from attorneys telephoning to ask about procedures, for expedited schedules, about the disposition of motions, and various other questions. Like district court judges, bankruptcy judges differ in their attitudes about direct contact between the clerk and attorneys; the clerk's conduct will of course be governed by the instructions of the particular bankruptcy judge, but the sections of this book discussing appropriate conduct in such situations may be useful.

Some bankruptcy judges ride circuit. Law clerks to those judges usually have substantial duties in preparing for travel, including assembly of materials necessary for the trip such as appropriate portions of case records. The clerk will usually have extra duties in the additional places of holding court because the other staff available may not be as complete as in the home court.

§ 6. U.S. Magistrates

Before 1968, U.S. commissioners were responsible for issuing federal arrest and search warrants, holding preliminary hearings, and trying petty offenses with the consent of the defendant. In 1968, Congress abolished this office and assigned the duties performed by commissioners to a new class of parajudicial officers, U.S. magistrates. 28 U.S.C. §§ 631–639. The authority of magistrates now derives primarily from the Federal Magistrates Act of 1968, 28 U.S.C. § 631 et seq., as interpreted by Mathews v. Weber, 423 U.S. 261 (1976), and as amended several times since then. The Magistrates Act permits each district court to appoint full- and part-time magistrates in such numbers and locations as may be determined by the Judicial Conference of the United States.

The duties of a magistrate include:

1. Administering oaths on criminal complaints and affidavits in support of search warrants;

2. Issuing arrest warrants or summonses upon a finding of probable cause in a criminal complaint;

3. Issuing search warrants upon a finding of probable cause from the affidavit in support of the application;

4. Acting as committing officer for persons arrested with or without warrant and advising the person arrested of that person's rights;

5. Conducting preliminary hearings in criminal cases to determine whether there is probable cause to believe that an offense has been committed and that the defendant has committed it; and

6. Appointing counsel and setting bail and conditions of release under 18 U.S.C. § 3142.

In addition, to the extent authorized by the appointing court, a magistrate may, pursuant to 28 U.S.C. § 636:

1. Try persons accused of, and sentence persons convicted of, misdemeanors when specifically designated to do so by the district court, 28 U.S.C. § 636(a)(3), 18 U.S.C. § 3401, unless the defendant elects to be tried before a district judge. A federal misdemeanor is an offense for which the maximum penalty is no more than one year's imprisonment. See also the *Rules of Procedure for the Trial of Minor Offenses Before United States Magistrates* promulgated by the Supreme Court on June 1, 1980, and reprinted as part of the one-volume edition of title 18 prepared by West Publishing Co. and available in each judge's chambers.

2. Serve as special master in civil actions and in proceedings pursuant to 28 U.S.C. §§ 2254 and 2255 when designated to do so by the district court;

3. Assist a district judge in the conduct of civil and criminal pretrial or discovery proceedings;

4. Perform a preliminary review of applications for post-conviction relief and make recommendations to facilitate the decision of the district judge to whom an application has been assigned; and

5. Serve as a judge for the trial of civil cases if all parties consent.

The local rules of court for each district describe the assignments that may be made to magistrates, and, therefore, the actual duties performed by magistrates in a particular court are determined by that court. In some courts, magistrates are utilized to the full extent permitted by the statute. In others, their duties are less extensive. The clerk for a district judge should examine the local rules of court and, by questioning others, ascertain the procedure of the court in this regard.

A district's full-time magistrates are appointed for a term of eight years by a majority of the judges of the district. Part-time magistrates are appointed for a term of four years. A magistrate may be removed from office by a majority of the judges of the district for incompetency, misconduct, neglect of duty, or physical or mental disability.

To qualify for appointment as a magistrate a person must be under 70 years of age, a member of the bar in good standing of the area to be served, competent to perform the duties of the office, and unrelated by blood or marriage to any judge of the appointing court. Some district courts impose additional requirements, such as a minimum number of years in law practice.

§ 7. Case Management: The Appellate Court

Each appellate court has a system for assigning cases, managing motions, and scheduling hearings. Because appellate courts do not take evidence or utilize jurors, the processes are simpler than in trial courts.

Federal appellate courts are required by statute to publish their internal operating procedures, and each law clerk should be certain to consult the local procedures.

MOTIONS

The processing of motions on appeal is described in the appellate court's internal operating procedures. Fed. R. App. P. 27 describes the prescribed form for motions. Some motions are decided by the clerk of court, some by a single judge, and some by a panel of judges. The local rules list those motions on which a single judge or the clerk of court has authority to act. Circuits differ on whether oral argument is heard on motions. In some circuits, there is no procedure for oral argument of a motion, unless specially requested by the court, and in other circuits substantive motions, such as those for bail, stays, injunctions, dismissal, or remand, are heard weekly as a matter of course.

SCREENING

Fed. R. App. P. 34(a) provides that oral argument shall be allowed in all cases unless pursuant to local rule a panel of three judges, after examination of the briefs and record, unanimously decides that oral argument is not needed. Oral argument is to be allowed "unless (1) the appeal is frivolous; or (2) the dispositive issue or set of issues has been recently authoritatively decided; or (3) the facts and legal arguments are adequately presented in the briefs and record and the decisional process would not be significantly aided by oral argument." Fed. R. App. P. 34. Pursuant to this rule most circuits employ a procedure known as "screening" to select those cases to be decided without oral argument, i.e., on the briefs alone. When the last brief is filed, the case is sent to a judge (or to a staff attorney) for screening classification. The policy in various circuits differs, but, for example, the Fifth and Eleventh Circuit Courts of Appeals both require that for oral argument to be denied all three judges of a screening panel must concur on three matters: (1) that oral argument is not required; (2) the result; and (3) the full text of the opinion, without separate concurrences. If all three criteria are met, the case is decided on the briefs, the appendix or record excerpts, and the record. For an example of a local rule, see the Fifth Circuit's Local Rule 34. See also J. Cecil and D. Stienstra, *Deciding Cases Without Argument: An Examination of Practices in Four Courts of Appeals* (Federal Judicial Center 1987), discussing procedures in the Third, Fifth, Sixth, and Ninth Circuits.

The screening process may also lead the court to conclude that the case is of special importance and warrants more than the time usually allowed for oral argument. The panel may then set it for an extended oral argument and notify counsel that additional time has been allowed.

Other methods are used to expedite the court's caseload. In response to the large number of appeals being filed, the Second Circuit in 1974 adopted a Civil Appeals Management Plan (CAMP) providing for a program of preargument conferences pursuant to Fed. R. App. P. 33. The purpose of the CAMP procedure is to encourage parties in civil cases to reach voluntary settlements early in the appellate process and, in those that do not settle, to improve the quality of briefs and arguments and resolve procedural problems. The preargument conference is conducted by the staff counsel. *A Reevaluation of the Civil Appeals Management Plan* (Federal Judicial Center 1983) provides an extensive explanation of the purpose and mechanics of the preargument conference. A number of the circuits have also adopted some form of preargument conference procedure, although the procedures differ considerably in purpose and method.

ORDER OF ASSIGNMENT OF CASES FOR ORAL ARGUMENT: CALENDAR PREPARATION

Ordinarily a case is not assigned to a particular panel of judges until it is scheduled for hearing. Once a case is assigned to a panel all motions are acted upon by the hearing panel rather than by a motions panel.

In most courts of appeals, one person, usually the clerk of court, selects the cases to be heard during a particular session of court without knowing which judges will be sitting. At the same time, someone else, usually the chief judge or a committee of judges, assigns the judges who will sit at that session without knowing which cases will be heard. Thus the judges' workload is equalized, but no person can influence the assignment of a case to a particular judge or panel of judges.

Courts that sit in more than one location within the circuit try to schedule a case for hearing at the location that is most convenient to counsel. In the Tenth Circuit, for example, a case in which all counsel have offices in Oklahoma will be scheduled for hearing in Oklahoma City if that scheduling will not create undue delay in the final disposition of the case.

When scheduling cases for a particular session, the person making the assignments operates under guidelines established by the court as to the number and kinds of cases to be scheduled for each day. In some courts an effort is made to equalize the workload for each day of the session and, if more than one panel is sitting, to equalize the workload among the panels. In others, the effort is only to equalize the workload for a week of sitting. In some circuits the person making the assignments also schedules cases with related issues or facts for the same panel. Alternatively, if a controlling case is awaiting decision by another panel in the court, the hearing may be delayed until the controlling case is decided. In most circuits the fact that the Supreme Court has granted certiorari in a case presenting the same issue is not considered sufficient reason to postpone assignment although the panel may, after hearing argument, decide to await the Supreme Court's decision before preparing an opinion.

The senior active judge on the panel is the presiding judge. During the course of a hearing, the court is under the control of the presiding judge. The crier, under the supervision of the judge, opens and closes court and maintains order and decorum.

The General Services Administration provides janitorial and maintenance services to the court. Each judge's law clerk or the crier has responsibility for supplying the courtroom with paper, pencils, drinking water, and other materials needed by the judge and counsel.

Each court has its own rules and customs regarding protocol, dress requirements, and courtroom behavior.

Courts of appeal do not have reporters, although they tape-record oral argument for the use of the court. Litigants who wish to have transcripts must request court approval and arrange for a reporter or some other person to prepare the transcript. Many courts maintain lists of qualified persons for this purpose.

ORDER OF OPINION WRITING

Although there is no statutory requirement that opinions be issued within a fixed time or in any particular order, most judges give priority to the preparation of initial drafts of opinions based upon three general criteria: (1) the importance and urgency of the decision; (2) the nature of the case, giving direct criminal appeals priority over civil cases; and (3) the order in which cases were argued to the court (or in which briefing was completed).

At any time, each judge will have drafts of opinions in various stages of preparation, and the length of time between preparation of the initial draft and issuance of the final opinion varies greatly depending upon the number of issues that must be treated, the complexity of those issues, the extent of suggested revisions and additions by other members of the appellate panel, and whether concurring or dissenting opinions will also be issued.

The Internal Operating Procedures of most courts include rules concerning the maximum time that should elapse before a proposed opinion is issued to other members of the panel by the writing judge and within which those panel members should respond. Each law clerk should become familiar with these rules.

DISTRIBUTING OPINIONS

After the opinion is issued, the original is filed with the clerk of court. When the opinion is filed, the clerk of court prepares a judgment in accordance with the operative language of the opinion. Fed. R. App. P. 36. The judgment is usually quite simple and merely reflects whether the judgment of the trial court is affirmed, reversed, or otherwise modified.

In most appellate courts, the clerk of court arranges for reproduction or printing of the opinion and distributes the copies. In some circuits, the typed opinion is sent to a printer by the clerk and the printer distributes the copies, called "slip opinions." Reproduction is usually accomplished through private contract printers, but may be done in-house by members of the clerk of court's office staff. (If a printer is used, the printer usually provides galley proofs of the slip opinion, which are proofread by the authoring judge's secretary or law clerks.) The slip opinions of several circuits are reproduced by West Publishing Co. In those circuits for which it is not the official printer, West Publishing Co. prepares its copy for publication in the *Federal Reporter 2d* and sends galley proofs to the authoring judge. The judge's secretary or law clerks proofread the galleys, make any necessary changes, and then return them to West for publication. These steps are eliminated in the circuits for which West is the slip opinion publisher. In those circuits, editorial changes are made on the slip opinion.

The clerk distributes copies of the final slip opinion to the parties, to all judges in the circuit, to traditional and computer on-line publishers, and to a large number of subscribers including government agencies, law offices, and law schools. In those circuits in which West Publishing Co. is the official printer, it mails these copies.

§ 8. Relations with Other Personnel and Their Functions: The Trial Court

(Note: Much in this section applies to clerks to bankruptcy judges. However, note the section on "Special Duties of Clerks to Bankruptcy Judges," p. 104.)

The clerk works closely with the other members of the judge's staff. The clerk also works with members of the staff of the clerk of court. The clerk for a district or bankruptcy judge will also have occasion to communicate with the marshal's staff, the probation office, the magistrates, and their clerical assistants. Law clerks also have frequent contact with the other judges of the court, their staffs, and the personnel of other agencies. Clerks should try to become acquainted with all their colleagues in the court.

Most of the non-judicial personnel who work for the courts are professionals or paraprofessionals in their own specialized areas. They can be of great assistance to a law clerk undertaking a task on behalf of a judge because they are permanent personnel and are familiar with the administration of their individual court. They should under all circumstances be treated with the respect they deserve. A friendly and helpful attitude toward all of the persons in the judicial system helps to develop efficient and pleasant working conditions.

The clerk for a district judge should visit the office of the clerk of court soon after reporting to work and ask the courtroom deputy assigned to the judge to explain the records kept, the duties of personnel in the clerk's office, and the procedures that lawyers must follow in filing materials.

Some courts have an orientation program for new clerks. The clerk should ask the judge or the judge's secretary whether such a program will be held and about the best way of meeting members of the court staff.

THE CLERK OF COURT

The clerk of a United States district court is appointed by and serves at the pleasure of the court. The clerk of court serves as the executive officer of the court (unless the court is served by a district court executive—see the next section) and manages a variety of complex, non-judicial functions delegated by the court. These responsibilities include:

1. Recruiting, hiring, classifying, training, and managing the staff;

2. Developing and implementing a records management system to properly maintain and safeguard the official records of the court;

3. Developing and maintaining a system to ensure the proper collection, accounting, and disbursement of funds and securities in the court's custody;

4. Developing budgetary estimates of future staffing requirements and other substantive expense items such as supplies, equipment, furniture, services, and travel;

5. Collecting and analyzing statistical data that reflect the performance of the court;

6. Managing the jury selection process, including the responsibility for making a continuing evaluation of juror utilization;

7. Maintaining liaison with all branches of the court and related government agencies;

8. Preparing and disseminating reports, bulletins, and other official information concerning the work of the court; and

9. Coordinating the construction of court facilities and periodically inspecting such facilities.

DISTRICT COURT EXECUTIVES

In an experimental program, some of the largest federal district courts have been allowed to appoint district court executives. In those courts, the executive performs the overall management responsibilities that would otherwise be assigned to the clerk of court, and the clerk's duties are those related primarily to the management and monitoring of the cases filed with the court.

THE PROBATION OFFICE

Each district court may appoint one or more probation officers, and, if more than one probation officer is appointed, the district court may also appoint a chief probation officer to supervise the activities of the other officers. Probation officers serve at the pleasure of the court. Their salaries are set by the director of the Administrative Office under the supervision and direction of the Judicial Conference.

The responsibilities and duties of a probation officer include:

1. Conducting presentence investigations and preparing reports on them for district courts, including reports for sentencing under the Sentencing Guidelines as required by the Sentencing Reform Act of 1984.

2. Completing investigations, evaluations, and recommendations to the court concerning alleged probation or supervised release violators;

3. Completing investigations, evaluations, and reports to the Parole Commission when parole is being considered for an offender;

4. Completing investigations, evaluations, and recommendations to the Parole Board concerning alleged parole violators;

5. Completing investigations, evaluations, and reports to the Parole Commission on matters pertaining to determination of indeterminate sentences given under the now-repealed Federal Youth Corrections Act, 18 U.S.C. § 5005;

6. Completing such duties as may be requested concerning the investigation and supervision of military parolees;

7. Providing the same service to U.S. magistrates as furnished to the district judges, when requested;

8. Supervising persons on probation, parole, supervised release, mandatory release, and military parole; and

9. Developing and investigating community plans for persons to be released from federal or military correctional institutions on parole or mandatory release, or supervised release.

By statute, U.S. probation officers have also been parole officers, although the officers' parole-related duties (see items 3 through 5 in the list above) will decline under the Sentencing Reform Act of

1984, which abolished parole for crimes committed after the effective date of the Act, November 1, 1987. See 18 U.S.C. § 3655.

THE PRETRIAL SERVICES OFFICE

The 1982 Pretrial Services Act directed that pretrial services be provided in all federal judicial districts. Pretrial services include evaluating persons proposed for pretrial release, monitoring and assisting those released, and reporting to the court on these activities (see 18 U.S.C. § 3154). Some district courts (including many small districts) provide pretrial services through their probation office; others have separate pretrial offices.

The circuit council must approve creation of a separate office, and the chief pretrial services officer is selected by a panel composed of the chief circuit and chief district judges and a magistrate, or their designees. The chief pretrial services officer appoints other officers with the court's approval.

THE JUDGE'S SECRETARY

In addition to traditional secretarial duties, a judge's secretary assists in maintaining the judge's calendar of assigned cases, serves as receptionist, deals with lawyers and members of the public on behalf of the judge, and manages the judge's office. The secretary's familiarity with the judge's office procedures and preferences is particularly helpful to a new clerk. The *Handbook for Federal Judges' Secretaries* (rev. 1985), published by the Federal Judicial Center and available in each judge's chambers, provides helpful information on the secretaries' duties and many of the policies of which clerks should also be aware. The secretary has many tasks; law clerks should be ready to assist whenever possible, for example, by answering the telephone when the secretary is busy or on another line.

THE JUDGE'S OTHER CLERKS

In most courts all clerks perform the same functions. Some judges have one permanent clerk and another with a one- or two-year commitment, in which case the permanent clerk may play a more significant role than the rotating clerk because the permanent clerk is already thoroughly familiar with the judge's practices and office administration. Most district judges, however, no longer have a permanent clerk.

Each judge has an individual system for making work assignments to clerks, but each makes an effort to balance the workload. In order to equalize the work between the clerks, allocations may be made on the basis of how much work will be required on a particular case. If a clerk has a preference for a particular subject matter, many judges try to accommodate that preference.

Although there may sometimes be salary differences between clerks (e.g., if one clerk is in a second year of clerking and the other is in the first year of clerking), the responsibilities of the clerks are usually the same. In district courts, the clerks may exchange the primary responsibility for administrative matters such as opening court, assembling files and records for the motion day, or preparing the conference room for a pretrial conference in alternate weeks. Such assignments are not rigid but are flexible, and each clerk should be cooperative in assisting the others when there is more work than can readily be completed in the time available.

THE COURTROOM DEPUTY

The duties and responsibilities assigned to courtroom deputies vary significantly from court to court and chambers to chambers depending upon the desires of the judges. The deputy, sometimes called a "minute clerk" or even "case manager," is an employee of the clerk of court's office, although the deputy may have a desk in the chambers of the judge to whom the deputy is assigned.

Nearly all courtroom deputies record the minutes of the court and assist the judge with control of the calendar for the scheduling of trials or hearings on motions. The deputy must keep the judge aware of all relevant information concerning the state of the calendar. The deputy also schedules the appearance of attorneys for hearings.

Other duties of courtroom deputies include:

1. Administering oaths to jurors, witnesses, and interpreters;

2. Maintaining custody of trial exhibits;

3. Entering or causing to be entered on the permanent records of the clerk's office a description of all relevant actions taken in open court or in chambers (usually called a minute entry);

4. Serving as liaison between the courtroom and the clerk of court's office; and

5. Performing routine clerk's office duties as needed and when available.

THE DOCKET OR MINUTE CLERK

The docket clerk works in the office of the clerk of court, and is responsible for maintaining the official records for each case pending before the judge. The docket clerk records on docket sheets (kept separately from the official record in a case) every pleading of any nature filed with the clerk of court with respect to a particular case. The docket clerk has custody of the official records and anyone who wants to review a record must request the record from the docket clerk. Save by order of the court or the clerk, a record may be taken from the clerk of court's office only by the judge. Some docket clerks have responsibility for assembling the records of cases to be heard at motion day or at trial. Usually, the docket clerk has the primary responsibility for knowing where the record is.

THE COURT REPORTER

Each district court has one or more court reporters; the number authorized for a court is determined by the Judicial Conference of the United States. Judicial Conference policy requires court reporters to work for the court (in a pooling arrangement) rather than for individual judges, although the implementation of this arrangement will vary with the number of judges and the places of holding court in the district. In practice, in some courts individual court reporters often work primarily in the courtroom of a specific judge, but a court reporter must adhere to the court's plan for pooling reporters and is not assigned to work only for a specific judge.

The duties of the court reporter include:

1. Recording all court proceedings verbatim by shorthand or by mechanical means;

2. Transcribing all arraignments, pleas, and proceedings in connection with the imposition of sentence in criminal cases, or filing a voice or sound recording of the proceedings, 28 U.S.C. § 753; and

3. Transcribing any proceedings upon request of a judge or any party to a proceeding.

The court reporter receives a salary, the amount of which is fixed by the Judicial Conference of the United States. Court reporters must provide their equipment and supplies at their own expense. In addition to salary, however, the reporter receives fees from litigants, including the United States, for transcripts requested by litigants and prepared by the reporter. The rate of the charge for transcripts is based on the number of pages transcribed and is prescribed by the court subject to the approval of the Judicial Conference. Transcripts are usually prepared only after a trial is completed and an appeal filed. Litigants may, however, request daily transcripts by notice in advance. If they do so, the reporter arranges for assistance from other reporters, because each can take and transcribe only a few hours of the proceeding in that limited time. The reporters make an extra charge for this service, which is paid by the litigants. That charge too is regulated by the court, subject to maximum limits set by the Judicial Conference.

The reporter must file a copy of every transcript with the clerk of the court. This is a public record that may be inspected by any person without charge during the business hours of the clerk's office.

If they wish, and subject to Judicial Conference regulations, district judges may direct the record to be taken by electronic sound recording rather than by a court reporter. If the court does so, an employee of the clerk of court is responsible for operating the equipment and seeing to the preparation of any requested transcripts.

SPECIAL MASTERS AND COURT-APPOINTED EXPERTS

Fed. R. Civ. P. 53 authorizes any district judge before whom an action is pending to appoint a special master. The term "special master" refers to an impartial expert who is designated to hear or consider evidence or to make an examination with respect to some issue in a pending action, and make a report to the court. A special master may be appointed in either a jury or a non-jury matter.

A referral to a special master may be expensive and time-consuming. Rule 53 states that referral to a special master "shall be the exception and not the rule." Litigants are entitled to a trial of every issue in court unless an "exceptional condition" is shown. Yet when issues in a jury case are so complicated that the court believes laymen are incapable of dealing with them unaided, the court may enlist the aid of a master to make findings on specific issues. In a jury case, these findings are admissible as "evidence of the matters found." The special master may be called to testify in the cause, and if called is subject to cross-examination, like any other expert. The court may also appoint a special master to assist the court in cases tried to the bench when the complexity of the case requires.

Any person who has particular competence to consider a complex matter may be appointed; thus a master may be a certified public accountant, an appraiser, or an economist. The compensation to be paid a special master is determined by the court and taxed as costs.

Magistrates may serve as special masters when appointed by the court pursuant to rule of court, 28 U.S.C. § 636. Their services as special masters are particularly helpful because they are officers of the court, they have experience in fact-finding and judicial procedures, and their appointment does not add to the expense of litigation because they are not paid extra compensation.

Fed. R. Evid. 706 authorizes the court to appoint expert witnesses. Such witnesses may be particularly helpful to the court and the jury when the experts who will testify for the opposing sides have rendered such diametrically opposite views on a matter that the judge thinks they are being advocates rather than impartial witnesses. The compensation of such expert witnesses is taxed against the parties in civil actions in the proportion the court directs. In criminal cases and civil cases involving just compensation under the Fifth Amendment, the expert's compensation may be paid with government funds.

STAFF LEGAL ASSISTANTS

In 1966, 8,540 prisoner actions of various kinds were filed in the district courts, 2,292 by federal prisoners and 6,248 by state prisoners. By 1976, 19,809 were filed, of which 4,780 were by federal prisoners, and by 1986, the district courts received 33,765 such petitions—4,432 from federal prisoners and 29,333 from state prisoners.

District courts with heavy prisoner filings may appoint law clerks to review the petitions, particularly pro se petitions, and prepare them for judicial action. Their work is not necessarily limited to filings under 42 U.S.C. § 1983.

§ 9. Relations with Other Personnel and Their Functions: The Appellate Court

THE APPELLATE CLERK'S OFFICE

Each court of appeals has a clerk who is appointed by and serves at the pleasure of the court. The clerk of court may be a lawyer, but a law degree is not a requisite for appointment. The clerk of court appoints necessary deputies and clerical assistants with the approval of the court. The number of employees authorized and their salary schedules are established by the Administrative Office.

The primary duties and responsibilities of a court of appeals clerk are:

1. Maintaining the files and records of the court;
2. Ensuring that all papers filed comply with the Federal Rules of Appellate Procedure and the rules of the court;
3. Entering all orders and judgments of the court;
4. Scheduling cases for hearing under guidelines established by law, rules, and orders of the court;
5. Distributing needed case materials to the members of the court;
6. Collecting, disbursing, and accounting for required fees;
7. Arranging for reproduction and distribution of the court's opinions;
8. Giving procedural assistance to attorneys and litigants;

9. Maintaining the roster of attorneys admitted to practice before the court;

10. Administering oaths;

11. Providing clerical staff for courtroom services; and

12. Providing necessary statistical case information to the court and the Administrative Office.

In addition the court may authorize the clerk of court to act on certain kinds of uncontested procedural motions. If the judge approves, each appellate law clerk should communicate with the clerk of court or the chief deputy soon after the clerkship begins in order to arrange a visit to the clerk's office. During such a visit the law clerk can meet the persons with whom the clerk may be working and can learn the procedure for carrying out such tasks as getting the record in a case.

THE CIRCUIT EXECUTIVE

The tasks of a circuit executive are assigned by the circuit council and are exercised under the supervision of the chief circuit judge. Although the specific functions may vary, the executive is usually responsible for a range of standard non-judicial administrative tasks, especially oversight of the personnel system and the budget for the court of appeals. The executive is the circuit's liaison to state courts, bar groups, the media, and the public. The circuit executive also collects statistical data on the flow and management of cases within the circuit and prepares reports for the circuit and for the Administrative Office. Because the executive's functions are generally administrative, a clerk will infrequently have any need to communicate with the circuit executive, except when delivering a message for the judge.

THE JUDGE'S SECRETARY

Each active appellate judge is authorized to employ two secretaries, one of whom is called the secretary and the other the assistant secretary. Their functions are similar to the functions of a secretary at the district court level, discussed at p. 115. The secretaries handle correspondence, do filing, type opinions, and maintain a log showing the status of all cases being handled by the judge. Many appellate judges also delegate internal administrative responsibility to their secretaries. Some judges require their clerks to type initial or rough drafts of opinions and internal office memoranda in order to reduce the volume of work that must be done by the secretaries.

THE LIBRARIAN

Each court of appeals maintains a library at its headquarters and additional branch libraries at other locations in those circuits that have jurisdiction over a large geographic area. These libraries are primarily for the use of the judges and their staffs, but are generally open to members of the bar, other governmental agencies, and the public.

Each library is managed by a librarian who is appointed by and serves at the pleasure of the court. The librarian may be responsible to the chief judge, a committee of judges, the circuit executive, or the clerk, as determined by the court.

In addition to the usual responsibilities involved in managing a library, some librarians publish a periodic newsletter describing new publications and acquisitions and listing books and articles of particular interest to their court. They may also make recommendations for new acquisitions to the library or, in some circuits, act on the recommendations of the judge responsible for recommending additions to the library.

Each circuit library has one or more staff members who have special training in legal research. These staff members can help clerks and judges in research. In some circuits the library staff will, for example, prepare a legislative history of a statute for a judge upon request.

The circuit library also has facilities for computerized legal research, including WESTLAW and LEXIS, and for general research on NEXIS. If the judge is not in a city that has a main or branch library with such facilities, it is likely that the main library has a staff member who, upon request, will execute computer research and furnish the results by telephone or mail. Most librarians will mail books to a judge or a law clerk working in another city or will photocopy materials needed for research. They will also try to obtain books not available in their libraries by borrowing them from other libraries. Clerks whose chambers are in a city where such a library is situated will find it advantageous to use it frequently. The circuit libraries have many more volumes than the judge's smaller working library.

The Law Library of the Library of Congress offers limited photocopying and research assistance to federal judges. The Law Library can compile indexes to federal legislative histories. Computerized data bases of current legislative materials, including the *Congressional Record,* are available, as well as rare treatises and extensive collections of American and foreign law periodicals. The Law Library can also perform bibliographic searches on specific subjects, though the personnel are not in a position to do extensive research. To request materials a law clerk or a judge should call the Chief of the American–British Law Division of the Law Library, Library of Congress, Washington, D.C. 20540.

THE STAFF ATTORNEYS

Each circuit now has a staff attorneys' office employing as many lawyers as the circuit has active appellate judges. Owing to its size, the Ninth Circuit has a somewhat larger staff. The administrative manager of the office is usually called the director of the staff attorneys' office or the senior staff attorney. One or more of the other staff members may also be assigned supervisory duties. The duties assigned to the staff attorneys' office vary from circuit to circuit, but in each circuit that office performs some or all of the following functions:

1. Reviewing correspondence from litigants (usually appearing pro se) in order to determine whether the correspondence is legally sufficient to constitute an appeal or a request for mandamus. Many of the letters or purported pleadings received by the court consist of handwritten papers, incomplete, difficult to read and to understand, prepared by a prisoner without legal assistance. When deciphered, they may be sufficient to constitute an appeal or petition for writs. If the correspondence, however, does not suffice to present an issue that may be considered by the court, the staff attorney may be authorized to so advise the author. If the correspondence is sufficient to invoke the

court's jurisdiction, the staff attorney is usually directed to prepare a memorandum stating the issues in the case and, after doing any necessary research, brief the legal issues.

2. Reviewing appeals and applications for mandamus involving collateral attack on state or federal criminal convictions. The staff attorneys' office usually reviews each such petition, analyzes the legal issues, prepares a memorandum of law concerning each issue raised, and recommends the disposition of the case. In some instances, the district court may have denied the certificate of probable cause that is the prerequisite for an appeal in forma pauperis, or may have failed to act on a request for such a certificate. If so, the staff attorney makes a recommendation concerning whether such a certificate should be issued. In many instances, the case will be sent to a panel of the court for decision on the merits without oral argument. In others, when the appellant is proceeding pro se, the staff attorney may recommend to the panel of judges to whom the case will be assigned that counsel be appointed. A panel of the court, however, makes the final decision in each case.

3. Preparing memoranda of law concerning the issues in, and recommended disposition of, motions.

4. Preparing memoranda of law concerning the issues in, and recommended disposition of, some criminal and civil cases. Because of the volume of work, most courts assign this duty to staff attorneys only in those types of cases most likely to involve repetitive presentation of similar issues or relatively easier issues. All others are assigned directly to a panel of judges.

5. In some circuits, assisting in case management and in settlement procedures. The Second Circuit, for example, has a Civil Appeals Management Program directed by two staff attorneys. See p. 108.

6. In some circuits, dividing cases into various categories, based on their expected difficulty, so as to assist the person who assigns cases to panels in allocating the anticipated workload evenly.

7. Other duties assigned by the court.

The staff attorneys' office may work under the supervision of the chief judge, a committee of judges, a single judge, a senior attorney, the circuit executive, or the clerk of court. Some staff attorneys are employed for limited terms, one or two years in duration. Others serve for longer periods. All are staff law clerks, so judges frequently call the clerks who work in their chambers on their personal staff "elbow clerks." As law clerks, staff attorneys are professionals who are entitled to the same respect as "elbow clerks."

THE CRIER

Each court of appeals has authority to employ criers, who also serve as bailiffs and messengers. The crier attends sessions of court and announces openings of court, recesses, and adjournments. As bailiff, this employee maintains order in the courtroom under the direction of the presiding judge. The crier also provides messenger services as needed by members of the court.

In some courts, as an economy measure, law clerks serve as bailiffs. In these circuits, the presiding judge of each panel or a person in the clerk of court's office arranges for this duty to be rotated among the clerks for the three panel members.

§ 10. Functions of Related Agencies and Personnel

PUBLIC DEFENDERS

The Criminal Justice Act of 1964 requires each district to have a plan to ensure that federal defendants are not deprived of legal representation because they cannot afford it. 18 U.S.C. § 3006A.

In some districts this need is met entirely by assigning cases to private attorneys. Districts in which at least 200 appointments are made annually, however, may establish public defender organizations, or community defender organizations. Federal public defender organizations are staffed by attorneys who are federal employees; the chief federal public defender is appointed by the court of appeals. Community defender organizations are nonprofit defense-counsel-service groups authorized by the plan to provide representation. Even where these organizations exist, however, the Judicial Conference has required that private attorneys be assigned at least 25 percent of the cases in which defendants are entitled to representation. This assures that a cadre of competent persons will be available to represent defendants in cases in which the defender organization has a conflict of interest or, for some other reason, cannot provide representation.

Although federal public defender office attorneys and staff are federal employees, paid by funds administered by the Administrative Office, they are not part of the district court staff. Their location in the judicial branch is primarily for the purpose of administrative convenience.

U.S. ATTORNEY

Criminal cases account for more than 30 percent of the total caseload of the U.S. district courts, and civil cases in which the United States is a party constitute more than 25 percent of all civil cases filed. In all cases in which the United States is a party, a representative of the Department of Justice is the attorney for the government. The representative is usually the U.S. Attorney or an Assistant U.S. Attorney for the district in which the case is pending, but in some cases a special assistant from the Department of Justice may appear. In some situations, such as federal tax refund suits against the United States, a lawyer from the Department of Justice may have primary responsibility for defense of the case, and the U.S. Attorney may serve as co-counsel of record. When the government party is a federal agency, such as the Equal Employment Opportunity Commission, agency counsel will usually represent the agency.

Each judicial district has a U.S. Attorney who is appointed by the President with the advice and consent of the Senate. The U.S. Attorney is appointed for a term of four years, but is subject to removal by the President. If a vacancy exists in the office, the Attorney General may appoint a U.S. Attorney, but that person may not serve for more than 120 days from the date of appointment. If the vacancy remains, the district court for the district in which the vacancy exists may appoint a U.S. Attorney to serve until the President fills the vacancy. 28 U.S.C. § 546. Assistants to the U.S. Attorney are appointed by, and may be removed by, the Attorney General.

The authority of a U.S. Attorney is set forth in 28 U.S.C. § 547. The responsibilities of a U.S. Attorney generally include:

1. Prosecuting all criminal offenses against the United States;

2. Prosecuting or defending for the government all civil actions in which the United States is a party;

3. Representing collectors or other officers of the revenue or customs in actions brought against them for official acts; and

4. Maintaining proceedings for the collection of fines, penalties, and forfeitures owed to the United States.

In connection with prosecutorial duties, the U.S. Attorney is usually present during sessions of a federal grand jury but may not remain while the grand jury is deliberating or voting.

THE MARSHAL'S OFFICE AND COURT SECURITY

The President, with the advice and consent of the Senate, appoints for each judicial district a U.S. Marshal who serves for a term of four years, but who, like the U.S. Attorney, is subject to removal. The marshal appoints deputies whose employment is governed by civil service regulations. The district court for the district may appoint a marshal to serve until a vacancy is filled by presidential appointment.

The duties and responsibilities of a marshal are:

1. To serve the district court and the court of appeals when the court is sitting in that district;

2. To execute all writs, process, and orders issued under the authority of the United States, including those of the courts; and

3. To pay the salaries and expenses of U.S. attorneys and their staffs, circuit judges, district judges, court clerks, and the marshal's own staff.

The marshal also has custody of federal prisoners awaiting trial, sentence, or transportation to a penal institution after conviction. Marshals and their deputies are authorized to carry firearms and may make arrests without warrant within statutory and constitutional limits.

Marshals and their deputies may exercise the same powers as sheriffs of the state in which they are located in carrying out their duties.

The marshal, working with each district court's security committee, implements a court security plan providing basic security services to judges and supporting personnel. Each court of appeals has a court security officer. Because of budgetary cutbacks, there is concern in some courts that security may not always be totally adequate. Especially because they will often be in the courthouse after hours, clerks should become thoroughly familiar with the court's security plan and with steps to take in an emergency.

Court security plans prepared in each district with the approval of its security committee specify the marshal's responsibility for attending to the jury. In many places the marshal or the marshal's deputy is in complete charge of the jury. Law clerks are sometimes told to avoid all contact with the jurors. The law clerk should inquire about the special procedures in the court to gain familiarity with them.

The marshal's office may also maintain security in the courtroom by having a deputy present in court, and maintain office and building security. At the discretion of the court, the marshal may be required to have a deputy attend any session of court. Courtroom and courthouse security, however, is also governed in each court by the court security plan. For security purposes, some judges have buttons for emergency buzzers beneath their desks and beneath their benches in the court room; if the button is pressed, an alarm sounds in the marshal's office.

The parties themselves, rather than the marshal, are ordinarily responsible for the service of process and subpoenas in civil cases. Different rules apply to each. Fed. R. Civ. P. 4(c)(2)(B) provides that a *summons and complaint* shall be served by the marshal only on behalf of a person authorized to proceed in forma pauperis, on behalf of the United States or an officer or agency of the United States, or by order of the court in special cases. Fed. R. Civ. P. 45(c) authorizes the marshal to serve *subpoenas* in civil cases, but service by any other person who is not a party and who is not less than 18 years of age is permitted and indeed encouraged by many courts because of limitations on the marshal's budget.

FEDERAL BUREAU OF INVESTIGATION

The Federal Bureau of Investigation, a bureau of the Department of Justice, is the agency charged with primary responsibility for detecting and investigating crimes against the United States. The FBI has its headquarters in Washington, D.C., but maintains offices throughout the United States. It is headed by a director, appointed by the President for a term of 10 years.

Local offices have agents in charge, and their staffs include special agents, secretaries, and clerical employees. Special agents of the FBI frequently are witnesses in federal criminal trials.

There are several other federal investigatory and law enforcement agencies that are assigned specialized duties, such as protecting the President, investigating counterfeiting activities and dangerous drug violations, and handling matters arising under the revenue, customs, and immigration laws of the United States. Within their specialized areas, the relationship of these officers to the courts is similar to that of FBI agents.

FEDERAL BUREAU OF PRISONS

When the judge sentences a person convicted of a federal crime, the order of commitment merely consigns the defendant to the custody of the Attorney General. The judge may recommend a preferred place of imprisonment, but the Attorney General has the final authority to designate the actual place of confinement.

The Federal Bureau of Prisons manages the penal and correctional institutions maintained by the United States. Its director is appointed by the Attorney General. Each judge has a pamphlet describing all institutions maintained by the Bureau of Prisons, their facilities, and their programs.

In addition to managing and regulating these institutions, the Bureau must provide suitable quarters, care, subsistence, and safekeeping for all persons held under the authority of the United States; provide for the protection, instruction, and discipline of all persons charged with or convicted of offenses against the United States; and provide technical assistance to state and local correctional institutions and officials.

In most judicial districts, there is no federal jail for the confinement of persons awaiting trial or after sentencing, so federal prisoners are confined to a state institution, under a contractual arrangement.

A judge may permit a sentenced defendant to report directly to the place of confinement. This avoids interim detention in state institutions that may be crowded or otherwise undesirable, and saves the government the expense of transportation. If the prisoner is dangerous, is likely to escape, is unreliable, is not likely to report on time, or cannot afford transportation, the judge is likely to require the marshal to maintain custody of the prisoner and to transport the prisoner to the institution designated by the Bureau.

For further information, refer to *Federal Prison System Facilities,* a softbound book available through the Department of Justice, No. JUS-434 (FPS-P 10-1).

CHAPTER 5. LEGAL RESEARCH AND WRITING

No judge has time to review all of the authorities bearing on each legal principle at issue in a case; legal research is therefore the most important task of any law clerk. Having done the research, the clerk will usually relay the results to the judge in writing, either by a memo or a draft opinion. To perform this and the many other writing assignments that make up the clerk's job, the clerk must write well: clearly, concisely, logically. This chapter provides suggestions for the clerk's research and writing tasks.

§ 1. Legal Research

A professional and well-crafted judicial decision can be made only in the context of precedent; the clerk's role is to make sure the judge has the material with which to understand the existing jurisprudence related to the case. This cannot be accomplished by relying on the briefs and the lawyers' research, however eminent the lawyers may be. Adequate judicial research includes not only checking the authorities cited in the briefs to determine the relevance of the authorities and the accuracy of the citations, but also going beyond the briefs and conducting independent research in order to determine whether the lawyers have overlooked either any controlling precedent or any helpful authority that may not be precedential.

The following suggestions may be of assistance:

1. Understand the *purpose* of the research project. For example, the extent and depth of research for a bench memo is less than that for an opinion.

2. Understand the *facts*. Judges apply law to specific factual situations, and if the facts of prior cases are distin-

guishable, those decisions may have little relevance, even if the same legal principle is at issue.

3. Understand the *legal issue*. It helps to restate the issue in writing; articulation helps to clarify the issue and often indicates whether the researcher's understanding is adequate and precise.

   If the legal area in which the issue arises is an unfamiliar one, first perform a preliminary survey of the field utilizing secondary sources such as:

   a. specialized treatises and texts;

   b. casebooks;

   c. law review articles;

   d. loose-leaf services;

   e. ALR annotations (these can be particularly helpful; some experienced researchers also include ALR as an early step in any research project); and

   f. legal encyclopedias

   Verify all secondary-source statements of the law. It is sometimes difficult to distinguish the author's opinions from the decisions cited.

4. Identify useful West *key numbers* pertinent to the subject through:

   a. cases cited in the parties' briefs;

   b. cases or key numbers located through the preliminary survey of secondary sources referred to above; and

   c. examination of the appropriate key number outlines of the West Digest System.

5. Examine the *headnotes* under the identified key numbers in the *Modern Federal Practice Digest* or other appropriate digest to locate those cases that are apparently in point.

6. Use *computerized research*. If WESTLAW or LEXIS is available, search for additional authorities. Plan your search carefully in advance, however, to avoid using computer time wastefully.

7. In cases involving federal statutes, begin the process by examining the annotations to the appropriate statutes in

United States Code Annotated. In cases involving state statutes, refer to the annotations in the state-statute source.

8. *Read the opinions in full.* Carefully examine the actual opinions to determine their applicability to the problem.

9. Be careful to distinguish the *holding* of a case from dicta.

10. Read all *dissents* and *special concurrences.* Those special opinions may be particularly helpful in understanding complex or novel legal questions.

11. Find *binding precedent.* Distinguish carefully between controlling and persuasive precedents. A state court decision on a procedural matter is usually not binding on a federal court, but a substantive decision of a state court may be controlling in a diversity case.

    Check to find whether there is conflicting authority within the circuit.

12. *Shepardize* or *cite check* any cases found to be on point to locate or determine:

    a. more recent decisions;

    b. similar cases from a controlling jurisdiction;

    c. more authoritative or better reasoned decisions; and

    d. the continued authority of those cases found to be useful.

13. *Exhaust all sources.* In the event this process fails to turn up appropriate precedents, turn to secondary sources or Shepardize or cite check similar but non-controlling cases or analogous cases with the hope of locating more controlling precedents, or ones at least more similar to the one to be decided.

14. *Use legal indices.* It is frequently helpful to consult the *Index to Legal Periodicals* and the *Current Law Index* for:

    a. case notes on key decisions (these are listed separately by case name); and

    b. articles on critical problems.

15. Do not overlook the American Law Institute *Restatements of the Law,* both in final and draft form, and the model and

uniform codes. (The Uniform Acts can be found in Martindale–Hubbell.)

16. Consult the *librarian* if you need help. The librarian can be of great assistance, particularly in obtaining legislative histories, less frequently used reference works, and materials from other libraries.

17. Use the *judge's files*. If the judge maintains an indexed file of the judge's prior opinions (as many do), consult these files. They may be extremely helpful if they contain work on a case similar to the one being researched.

CURRENT ADVANCE SHEET AND SLIP SHEET READING

In addition to research on specific cases, law clerks have a professional responsibility to keep up with developments in the law. Read as promptly as possible all decisions of the Supreme Court. The judge will receive them first in *United States Law Week* and shortly thereafter in Supreme Court slip sheets. Both appellate and district court clerks must read all slip opinions issued by their circuit as soon as possible after they are received. They are mandatory precedent to district courts and law of the circuit for other panels of the circuit court. The clerk should immediately call to the judge's attention any opinion bearing on a currently pending case. District court clerks should also review all opinions of their district that appear in the advance sheets of the *Federal Supplement*.

If time permits, a clerk should also review decisions published in the *Federal Reporter* and *Federal Rules Decisions*. Because of the large number of opinions now being published, it may not be possible to read the full text of all opinions. After reviewing the headnote of each case, the clerk may choose to read in full at least those opinions applicable to cases pending before the judge, presenting issues commonly occurring in the court, and decisions otherwise of particular interest. District court clerks should also scan the state reporter, or regional reporter, for decisions by the courts of the state in which the judge sits, because the judge must apply substantive principles of state law in cases founded upon diversity jurisdiction.

§ 2. Writing

GENERAL RULES

Some judges do all of their own writing and rely upon their law clerks only to prepare memoranda to communicate the results of assigned research tasks within the office. Others expect their clerks to draft opinions and orders in final form, suitable for filing, if approved by the judge. Some judges assume personal responsibility for writing final opinions in cases that have been tried, but require their law clerks to prepare drafts of opinions disposing of preliminary motions. Regardless of the drafting process, decision-making remains exclusively the judge's responsibility.

A law clerk may be assigned writing tasks for some or all of these kinds of documents:

1. Memoranda to the judge;
2. In the district court, orders and minute entries; in the courts of appeals, orders and short per curiams or other brief dispositions.
3. In the district court, opinions including findings of fact and conclusions of law; in the courts of appeals, both memorandum orders and opinions; and
4. Correspondence.

Certain general rules of good writing style are applicable to all of these categories. They include:

1. *Prepare an outline before starting.* The best way to organize your thoughts and to be sure to include everything you want to say is to prepare a logical sentence or topical outline before beginning to write. Such an outline may not be necessary before preparing a short minute entry or order, but it is essential before writing a draft opinion or any long document.
2. *Introduce the subject.* At the outset, let the reader know what the subject of the document is. If you are preparing a memorandum on a specific issue, you should begin the memorandum with a precise statement of the issue, followed by your conclusions as to its resolution. If you are preparing an opinion or a memorandum summarizing an

entire case, you should identify the parties, explain at the outset the history of the case, state the issues and the resolution of them, and the action taken by the court, e.g., judgment vacated, motion for summary judgment denied, affirmed, etc.

3. *Avoid the use of generic terms as specific identifiers.* Fed. R. App. P. 28(d) states:

> Counsel will be expected in their briefs and oral arguments to keep to a minimum references to parties by such designations as "appellant" and "appellee." It promotes clarity to use the designations used in the lower court or in the agency proceedings, or the actual names of parties, or descriptive terms such as "the employee," "the injured persons," "the taxpayer," "the ship," "the stevedore," etc.

The same policy applies in district courts.

4. *Follow the proper format.* The judge may require a special organization and arrangement of intra-office written materials and may have standardized formats for other written materials. Learn these standard formats and follow them. The judge's files contain materials used in other cases that provide examples. The judge's secretary can also advise you whether the judge has a prescribed form.

5. *State the relevant and material facts.* To understand the application of legal principles to a case or an issue the reader must know the basic and significant facts of a case; do not include inconsequential information that does not bear directly on the question to be decided.

6. *Be accurate and give appropriate references.* Be careful to quote accurately from a cited authority. Be certain that cited authority has not been overruled or qualified.

Some judges require their clerks to give citations to the sources of factual statements. Thus, if a particular fact is established by Smith's deposition, its statement is followed with "(Smith depo. p. 10)." This reference allows the judge easily to locate and read the statement in context and verify its accuracy. Often, lawyers will support their statements of fact in a brief by citing a deposition, a transcript of trial, or an exhibit. You should verify those citations before incorporating them.

7. *Write succinctly, clearly, and precisely.* Good legal writing is simple, brief, and clear. Unnecessarily abstract or complex words and phrases, flowery language, or literary devices may interfere with the reader's ability to understand the point. Unless the judge instructs otherwise, leave embellishment to the judge.

8. *Subdivide.* In a lengthy opinion or order, the reader may find it easier to follow if the material is divided into subparts, each labeled with letters or numbers or short subtitles.

Editing

The four primary goals of editing are:

1. To correct errors in grammar and punctuation;

2. To eliminate ambiguities;

3. To improve the manner and order of presentation of the law or facts; and

4. To improve the writing style.

Editing includes deletion of words and phrases that may be misunderstood or may create confusion, the elimination of redundant material, and the correction of verbosity. Similar principles apply whether you are editing your own work or that of another clerk or the judge:

1. If you are editing your own work, you should set the draft aside and work on something else for a while before beginning editing. A fresh view may suggest improvements that may otherwise not occur to you.

2. Read the material to be edited aloud; this may disclose previously unnoticed problems.

3. If the judge has another law clerk, ask the co-clerk to read and comment on the draft, especially if that other clerk has not worked on it.

4. Brevity and clarity are both important. Clarity is often improved by the elimination of unnecessary elaboration.

5. Short, simple sentences are generally preferred to lengthy, compound, or complex sentences.

6. The use of excessive punctuation may indicate that the sentence should be broken into two or more sentences.

Style

Each judge has a different writing style. Some prefer simple declarative sentences and the use of plain language. Others employ complex sentences and a varied vocabulary. Some use metaphor and simile to make a point. Whatever the judge's personal style, most prefer that their law clerks not attempt to impose each clerk's own style on opinions and court documents, but instead try to write in the manner that the judge has adopted. The judge will continue to issue opinions year after year and abrupt changes in style from year to year are undesirable. Read several of the judge's prior opinions to become familiar to the judge's style. If in doubt, ask the judge what stylistic embellishment is desired.

The following are reference books that every judge and clerk should have:

1. R. Copperud, *American Usage and Style* (1980) (Van Nostrand Reinhold). This book presents the consensus of numerous usage authorities.

2. *Webster's New World Dictionary* (2d college ed. D. Duralnik 1978) or *The American Heritage Dictionary of the English Language* (W. Morris ed. 1978). As Copperud notes, these two dictionaries are "the most attentive to points of usage"; that is, they indicate levels of style or usage: nonstandard, informal, slang, vulgar, obsolete, and the like.

3. W. Strunk, *The Elements of Style* (3d ed. E. White 1979) (Macmillan). A classic. Particularly good for general advice on writing.

4. D. Lambuth, *The Golden Book of Writing* (1976) (Penguin). Similar to Strunk's book.

5. H. Fowler, *A Dictionary of Modern English Usage* (2d ed. E. Gowers 1965) (Oxford University Press).

6. W. Follett, *Modern American Usage* (J. Barzun ed. 1966) (Hill & Wang). More scholarly and detailed than Copperud (who, by the way, cites it frequently), but still invaluable. Widely recognized as one of the premier usage authorities.

7. *U.S. Government Printing Office Style Manual* (rev. ed. 1973). A comprehensive guide to capitalization, spelling, compounding (e.g., "fact finder," "fact-finder," or "factfinder"?), punctuation, abbreviations, numerals, and other matters of style.

8. *Harbrace College Handbook* (most recent edition).

9. *Webster's New Dictionary of Synonyms* (1978) (G. & C. Merriam). Splendid for distinguishing among synonyms (e.g., "language," "dialect," "tongue," "speech," and idiom, e.g., "let," "allow," "permit," "suffer," and "leave").

The following books will also be useful to judges and clerks:

1. T. Bernstein, *The Careful Writer* (paper ed. 1977) (Atheneum).

2. M. Freeman, *The Grammatical Lawyer* (1979) (American Law Institute).

3. J. Bremner, *Words on Words* (paper ed. 1980) (Columbia University Press).

4. R. Flesch, *The ABC of Style* (paper ed. 1964) (Perennial).

5. E. Partridge, *Usage and Abusage* (6th ed. 1965) (Hamish Hamilton (London)).

6. H. Weihofen, *Legal Writing Style* (1961) (West).

7. W. Morris and M. Morris, *Harper Dictionary of Contemporary Usage* (1985).

8. B. Evans & C. Evans, *A Dictionary of Contemporary American Usage* (1957) (Random House).

SPECIFIC WRITING ASSIGNMENTS

Jury Instructions

Most district judges expect their law clerks to assume a major role in preparing proposed jury instructions. Some judges send a written copy of the instructions to the jury room with the jury. If the judge does this, the instructions must be typed and ready before the end of the presentation of evidence. Judges who do not give the jury a written copy of the instructions may require a draft of the charges to be available for a charge conference just before the parties rest. In all cases the charges must be prepared promptly.

The judge will indicate whether the case will be submitted to the jury for a general verdict or on special interrogatories. The use of special interrogatories may substantially affect the content of the charge. In addition, the judge will decide whether the trial of one or more issues is to be separated; for example, it is common in tort cases to try the liability issue separately and to ask the jury first to reach a verdict on this issue. If the jury decides for the defendant, it will be unnecessary for it to decide damages. If it decides for the plaintiff, the parties may reach a compromise without going to trial on damages.

The judge will have instructed the trial counsel to submit requests for charges. Most local court rules require that proposed instructions be submitted in duplicate at the beginning of the trial or at some earlier time. They may, of course, be supplemented if unforeseen matters arise during the course of the trial. Counsel is instructed that each paragraph of a requested charge should be typed on a separate piece of plain white letter-sized paper with the description at the top and numbered, for example, as Plaintiff's Requested Jury Charge No. 1, with a citation of authority, such as a case or statute, at the end of the paragraph. (The citations are not read to the jury but enable the judge or clerk quickly to determine whether the charge is correct.) Most likely, the judge will review counsel's requested charges and will give the clerk preliminary reactions. The judge may also instruct the clerk to look for a standard charge or to consult the judge's office charge book. (See "Pattern or Previously Used Jury Instructions," p. 141.) In addition, the clerk should consult the record and the pretrial order, learn about the issues, and research the cases in order to prepare a draft of proposed charges. Substantive accuracy is of the utmost importance; a principal cause of reversals or new trials is substantive error in jury instructions.

Clear jury instructions require complete mastery of subject and the use of plain language. Each instruction should be written in short, simple sentences, enumerating the elements of a violation, theory, or defense so that the jurors can approach a decision step by step. Names and facts should be inserted where appropriate, and the pertinent statute or legal rule should be quoted in part or paraphrased. The instruction should state the applicable rule in a way that makes sense and should be written in language that a high school student could understand.

Fed. R. Civ. P. 51 and Fed. R. Crim. P. 30 require that the judge inform counsel before closing argument which jury charges will be given. Some judges hold a charge conference with counsel, usually in chambers, but on the record; discuss the proposed charge; and permit counsel to argue for their suggestions. Others do not hold a charge conference but deliver a copy of their proposed charges to all counsel and give counsel an opportunity to comment, object, or request additional charges in writing.

In any event, before the jury is instructed, each counsel must be given an opportunity in conference or in open court, but out of the presence of the jury, to make objections to the proposed charge. Some judges require counsel to write their objections directly on a copy of the proposed charge and then file this copy in the record for purposes of appellate review. If changes are made after a lawyer voices objections, the charges are retyped and a copy of the charge as delivered is filed in the record. This procedure accurately records the charges requested, the objections made, if any, and the charge delivered, in order to provide a complete and accurate record to the appellate court.

Pattern or Previously Used Jury Instructions

Once a final set of jury instructions has been prepared for a specific type of case, a copy should be retained in the judge's office file on form jury instructions. Those instructions are the starting point for the next case involving similar issues. Form civil and criminal jury instructions may be kept in separate loose-leaf binders. In every court many cases present similar issues. Form jury instructions for such cases may be photocopied or mimeographed for distribution to the attorneys before they prepare suggested charges. For example, in the Eastern District of Louisiana, the number of actions involving seamen, the Jones Act, and unseaworthiness is large enough to justify preparation of standard form instructions. Whatever the nature of the case, preserving a copy of the instructions can save future work. If the judge has developed an instruction on the issues involved, e.g., an instruction on liability for committing fraud in the sale of securities in violation of Rule 10b-5 in a securities case, only slight modification of the standard charge to fit the names and circumstances of the present case should be required.

In 1988, the Federal Judicial Center published the *Pattern Criminal Jury Instructions,* developed by the Subcommittee on Pattern Jury Instructions of the former Judicial Conference Committee on the Operation of the Jury System. In several circuits, committees of district judges have developed pattern jury charges that serve as a helpful guide. Such charges have, for example, been prepared in the Fifth, Seventh, Ninth, and Eleventh Circuits. Each judge in those circuits has a copy of the pattern charges and most judges use them as a starting point.

For forms previously used by other district judges, many judges consult Devitt and Blackmar, *Federal Jury Practice and Instructions* (3d ed. 1977) (West). Another comprehensive work is *Modern Federal Jury Instructions,* edited by Judge Leonard B. Sand of the Southern District of New York and others. In antitrust cases, it may be useful to consult the American Bar Association's *Sample Jury Instructions in Civil Antitrust Cases* (1987). The ABA Litigation Section has prepared *Model Jury Instructions for Business Tort Litigation* (1980). In addition, many specialized texts include forms for jury charges in those legal fields.

Memoranda of Law or Fact

A memorandum is an informal document intended to communicate the results of a research assignment or a summary of a case. All memoranda should indicate:

a. The person by whom the memo was prepared (some judges wish the law clerk to use initials only);

b. The date it was prepared; and

c. The type of memo, or a short summary of the subject discussed.

Some of the most common memoranda are:

1. *The bench memorandum.* This is a document prepared by an appellate law clerk for the judge to use during oral argument. Most judges want bench memos to be brief, usually only a page or two, and do not require a significant amount of independent research by the law clerk. The bench memo is most often a summary of the briefs of the parties, together with (when requested) the clerk's analysis of the validity of the respective positions of the parties and identification of issues that require further inquiry.

One commonly used organizational format for a bench memo is:

a. the docket number, short caption of the case, and names of members of the panel;

b. the district court and the name of the judge from whom the appeal is taken;

c. a statement of the case, reflecting how the case arose, the trial court's ruling, and which party appealed;

d. a brief statement of the facts of the case;

e. a statement of the issues raised by the parties;

f. a summary of the arguments raised by the parties;

g. matters that should be clarified, expanded, or explained during oral argument; and

h. if requested by the judge, the clerk's views on the merits of the case, supported by analysis and explanation, and recommendations on disposition of the case. (Some judges do not wish their law clerks to express any views and others discourage any conclusionary language until after the case has been argued and thoroughly researched.)

2. *The statement of facts.* Frequently, a judge wants the facts in a particular case or the facts relating to a specific issue summarized in writing. In an appellate court the sources for this kind of memo are the briefs and appendix or record excerpts; in a trial court the sources are the case file, trial exhibits, the law clerk's notes taken during hearings, and, when necessary, the court reporter's notes or transcripts.

    In preparing a statement of facts the law clerk should strive for accuracy and objectivity, and, if there are disputed factual issues, the clerk must present the evidence supporting each position. The clerk should neither allow a personal opinion to shade the statement of facts nor present a partisan view of the evidence. A narrative statement of the facts, arranged chronologically, is usually the easiest to understand. Many judges wish the law clerk then to express a view about how any conflicts in the evidence should be resolved.

3. *The single-issue memorandum.* The need for a memo dealing with a single issue may arise from inadequate preparation by counsel, an unexpected development during trial, or the judge's wish to pursue an aspect of the case not fully developed by the attorneys. This memo may be prepared under extreme time pressure during trial, but nevertheless must be prepared with accuracy and care.

4. *The full-case memorandum.* This type of memo is usually preliminary to an opinion, and unless otherwise instructed, the law clerk should approach it in that manner. It is usually better to overwrite this kind of memo, including facts of borderline relevancy and legal research that, although not directly on point, may have some bearing on the outcome of the case. It is easier to delete unnecessary material than to insert material omitted from an earlier draft. Some judges like this memo prepared in the form of an opinion.

Legal Memoranda Files

Legal problems do repeat themselves. After completing a research memorandum, or upon reading a brief submitted to the court that is unusually thorough, the clerk should file a copy in the judge's legal memoranda files for future use. Such files can be an invaluable resource and prevent needless duplication of effort. Some judges maintain these files in expandable folders or manila folders filed in alphabetical order in a file drawer, labeled by subject. If the judge has a computer, it is useful to maintain a computerized index to these materials on the computer.

Resolution of Motions in Trial Courts

The resolution of motions often constitutes a substantial part of the trial court's work on a case. Some motions may require an opinion equivalent in substance and length to a final opinion after trial. In most, the judge may write only a short opinion or order, dictate reasons into the record, or simply indicate disposition in a single word: "Granted" or "Denied." The clerk is usually the member of the judge's staff charged with responsibility for knowing which motions are pending, what memoranda or other pleadings have been filed with respect to each motion, and the status of each such motion. The judge will instruct the clerk what type of memorandum or order is indicated. Motion management is discussed in more detail in Chapter 3.

Some judges wish their clerks to prepare a memorandum on every motion. Others require memoranda only on certain matters or for certain types of cases.

If required to prepare a memorandum, the clerk should first examine the briefs or memoranda from both the moving party and the opposition. Often the legal standard or rule that applies is fairly clear; the difficulty is in applying the legal rule to the facts, and the facts are almost always incompletely—sometimes even deceptively—presented. Each party's version must be examined and compared, and then checked against the exhibits, declarations, or materials in the record.

The clerk should find samples of predecessors' memos and use them as guides. There is no one style or format for memos on motions, but certain features are common:

1. Name and number of the case, perhaps the category of case (e.g., antitrust, diversity tort case), the date of the memo, and the writer's initials.

2. Statement of the nature of motion or motions now under consideration, identifying the moving party.
3. Recommended disposition, summarized.
4. Statement of facts and procedural posture. This should include a description of the parties and their relationships to one another, key events, and a notation of facts in dispute. The memo should indicate the source of the facts stated, particularly when they are controverted or perhaps intentionally vague, such as the paragraph of the complaint, the identification of the relevant affidavit and paragraph number, or the number of the exhibit from which the fact stated is derived.
5. Discussion of the parties' chief arguments, the legal standard set by controlling statutes, rules, or precedent, and a succinct explanation of the clerk's reasons for recommending a particular result on each point.
6. Some judges may wish to have a draft of a proposed order or judgment disposing of the matter along the lines recommended by the clerk.

When the memo is completed, the clerk should give it to the judge with the case work file, retaining a copy.

Memos for Criminal Motions

The law clerk is not usually required to prepare a memo for each motion in a criminal case. In some districts, motions are made in an omnibus pleading. In others, they may be made separately but without a predetermined schedule because the Speedy Trial Act requires that a criminal defendant go to trial within 70 days of the initiation of proceedings, and there is little time for briefing schedules.

Before writing a memorandum, the clerk should check with the courtroom deputy (or, if the judge's policy permits, with opposing counsel) to determine whether opposing counsel will oppose the motion. Many suppression motions, for example, are not contested. The judge may handle last-minute evidentiary or procedural motions personally, as they often surface first during the pretrial conference. When a memo must be written, though, the process is essentially the same as in preparing memos in civil cases.

Findings of Fact and Conclusions of Law

When a district court judge sits as the trier of fact in an evidentiary hearing or trial, the judge may prepare either an opinion of the conventional kind or findings of fact—a statement in separately numbered paragraphs of each ultimate fact that the judge concludes was proved. In the latter case the judge will also prepare conclusions of law; these follow the findings of fact and state in separate paragraphs the principles of law the judge concludes are applicable to the facts.

Arranging findings of fact and conclusions of law in separately numbered paragraphs (each consisting of one or two relatively brief declarative statements) assists the parties to understand the opinion and makes appellate review easier. The judge may direct the clerk to prepare a draft of either the opinion or the findings of fact and conclusions of law.

In some cases the court requires counsel for the plaintiff to prepare proposed findings of fact and conclusions of law and requires counsel for the defendant to respond to the plaintiff's proposals. Other judges may require each counsel to prepare separate proposals. The court then reviews the proposals and makes necessary revisions or additions before adopting any of them.

If proposed findings of fact are based on transcribed testimony (either by deposition or of the trial), the court may insert citations to page numbers of the various transcripts at the end of each paragraph of conclusions of fact, and the clerk may be asked to review those citations. The clerk may also be given the task of reviewing legal authorities cited by the parties in their trial briefs to determine whether the proposed conclusions of law are correct.

District Court Orders

Fed. R. Civ. P. 58 provides "upon a general verdict of a jury, or upon a decision by the court that a party shall receive only a sum certain or costs or that all relief shall be denied, the clerk [of court], unless the court otherwise orders, shall forthwith prepare, sign, and enter the judgment without awaiting any direction by the court." If, however, the court grants other relief, or the jury returns a special verdict or a general verdict accompanied by answers to interrogatories, the clerk of court prepares a form of judgment and "the court shall promptly approve the form of the judgment, and the clerk [of court] shall thereupon enter it." The rule also provides: "Attorneys shall not submit forms of judgment except upon direction of the court, and these directions shall not be given as a matter of course."

Routine orders are usually prepared in the office of the clerk of court. In some cases, however, it may be necessary for the court to prepare an order that states the relief to be granted. These orders are prepared in the judge's chambers, and are sometimes drafted by the clerk. In some courts and in some circumstances, the judge may direct the prevailing party to prepare an order and submit it to opposing counsel for approval.

Most courts have a standardized format for orders, and the judge's secretary will be familiar with that format. This usually includes the name of the court, the docket number of the case, the caption of the case with the names of the parties, and a descriptive title indicating the nature of the order. A paragraph should be included stating the date of the hearing, if any, appearances of counsel, and the nature of the matter decided by the order.

An order has two functional parts: (a) the factual or legal basis for the determination and (b) a statement that tells the parties what action the court is taking and what they must do as a result of that action.

No specific language is required to make an order effective. Use language that is simple and unambiguous. The purpose of the order is to tell the person to whom the order is directed precisely what to do and to allow others to determine whether that person has done it correctly and completely.

Reviewing Orders and Judgments Submitted by the Parties

The parties may submit proposed orders or judgments for the district judge's signature as a result of the following types of actions: (a) the judge has ruled from the bench on a legal matter and has asked the prevailing party to submit an appropriate order for the judge's signature; (b) the judge has decided a non-jury case, announced from the bench the judge's findings or reasons and grounds, and asked the prevailing party to submit an appropriate judgment; or (c) the parties have stipulated to a result in a particular case, with or without the judge's prior involvement, and have submitted a proposed order, accompanied by their stipulation, for the judge's approval and signature. In other cases, pursuant to Fed. R. Civ. P. 58, the clerk of court may submit a prepared form of judgment for court approval.

When these documents arrive at the chambers, the law clerk is usually responsible for their detailed review, and should take the following steps:

1. If the order or judgment is being submitted after the judge has made a determination in court with all parties present, the clerk should check to be certain that it has been approved as to form by the losing party; this means that the losing party agrees that the order or judgment conforms to the judge's decision. Such approval is usually indicated by the signatures of counsel for the losing party, e.g. "Approved as to form. Signed J. Attorney, Counsel for Defendant."

2. If the parties have agreed or stipulated to the decision, with or without the judge's prior involvement, the clerk should confirm that the submitted order or judgment is accompanied by the stipulation, signed by the parties, and the order or judgment itself has been approved as to *form* and *substance* by all parties.

3. The clerk should check the substance of the order or judgment to be certain that it complies with the judge's directions on the stipulation or agreement. The clerk should approach the judge with any question about the complete correctness of the order or judgment.

Opinions

1. *Research.* To write a draft of an opinion a clerk must first become thoroughly familiar with the case. Read the briefs and the record or case file, complete all necessary legal research, and discuss the proposed opinion with the judge, examining the structure, the rationale, and the result to be reached.

Frequently, additional research is necessary as the opinion is being drafted.

2. *Listening to tape recordings of oral arguments.* Many circuit courts record appellate oral arguments. Even the clerk who attended oral argument should listen to the tape before beginning to draft an opinion to refresh memory concerning the issues, the judges' questions to counsel, and counsel's responses. Moreover, because many clerkships are for single-year periods, a clerk may be assigned the task of drafting an opinion in a case in which oral argument was heard before the beginning of the clerk's tenure. In most circumstances, listening to the tape is essential.

In the district court, an audio recording of the trial may assist in reviewing the issues or preparing a draft opinion. Many court reporters tape record the trial as an aid in preparing the transcript; they may be willing to release this audio record to the clerk. For those courtrooms in which audio recording is the official court reporting method, the clerk of court can provide the tape recording.

Oral arguments on motions or legal questions in district court are usually not transcribed and do not ordinarily form part of the record. Unless the attorneys ask the court reporter to take down such oral arguments, no record will be available. In most appellate courts, the clerk of court makes a tape recording of all arguments, and this tape is provided to the judge assigned to write the opinion.

3. *Planning the opinion.*

   a. Write a clear statement of the facts presented in the case and the legal issues presented by them.

   b. Determine which issues must be decided. If the case turns on a procedural issue, any discussion of substantive issues raised by the parties may be gratuitous; occasionally, if the same result would have been reached after considering the substantive issues, so stating may strengthen the opinion.

   c. Determine which parts of the opinion raise issues to be treated in detail. If there is a circuit decision directly on point, a lengthy analysis of the precedents and principles involved in that particular issue has little value.

d. Outline the opinion. In opinions as in any other kind of writing, a good outline will help the writer produce a clear, complete, and well-organized product.

4. *Writing the opinion*

a. *The introduction, or opening paragraph.* The introduction should establish clearly who the parties are, and, if the case is on appeal, what agency or court decisions are being reviewed. In addition, many judges like to state at the outset the principal issue and the decision made by the writing court. This practice has the advantage of informing the reader of the result in the case immediately. Thus, the opinion of the Supreme Court in First English Evangelical Lutheran Church v. County of Los Angeles, 482 U.S. 304, 107 S. Ct. 2378, 96 L. Ed. 2d. 250 (1987), written by Chief Justice Rehnquist, begins:

> In this case the California Court of Appeal held that a landowner who claims that his property has been "taken" by a land-use regulation may not recover damages for the time before it is finally determined that the regulation constitutes a "taking" of his property. We disagree, and conclude that in these circumstances the Fifth and Fourteenth Amendments to the United States Constitution would require compensation for that period.

b. *The facts.* State the facts developed at the trial or in the record in chronological order. Do this in a narrative style, using short sentences. Recite all of the relevant facts but omit everything else. Avoid verbatim quotations of excerpts from the pleadings or the transcript. In an appellate opinion, this part of the opinion may conclude with a resume of the trial court's or agency's reason for its decision and a statement of the issues on appeal.

c. *Applicable law.* Discuss the legal principles applicable to the case. Avoid lengthy quotes from cases or treatises. Cite the authorities for these principles, but avoid string citations.

Meritless points do not require detailed discussion. Many lawyers will present a smorgasbord of issues in the briefs, hoping that the judge may find some tempting morsel among the offering. In such cases, mention these issues so the lawyers will know they were noticed and simply say they are without merit (e.g., "considering the testimony of the informant, the argument that the evidence was insufficient to warrant conviction merits no discussion.")

d. *Disposition.* Apply the legal principles to the facts.

e. *Closing.* Close with a specific statement of the disposition: judgment is rendered for the plaintiff in the amount of $X; the judgment appealed is affirmed; revised and rendered; or reversed and the case is remanded.

f. *Footnotes.* When reviewing a footnoted opinion, the reader's eyes must constantly move from text to footnotes and back again. This may distract the reader and waste time. For this reason, some judges object to any footnotes. Others use footnotes only for citations. Most judges use them to expand on the text of an opinion, to explain an inference in the opinion, or to discuss authorities. The law clerk should determine and, of course, follow the judge's practice.

g. *General suggestions.* Remember: This is a judicial opinion, not an essay or a law review article. Write simply. Stick to the active voice. Avoid excessive use of adjectives and adverbs. Make the meaning clear by using verbs and nouns. It is neither necessary nor desirable to cite every case you have read. Rewrite until the message is pared to essentials. The final result should be a cogent opinion that states the court's decision and the basis on which it was reached.

h. *References.* Good references to consult regarding the style of appellate court opinions are Witkin, *Appellate Court Opinions—A Syllabus for a Panel Discussion at the Appellate Judges' Conference,* 63 F.R.D. 515 (1966), and Leflar, *Appellate Judicial Opinions* (1974).

CORRESPONDENCE

Some district judges do not permit law clerks to correspond with lawyers in any case. Some draft all of their own correspondence or delegate this responsibility to their secretaries. Others direct their law clerks to prepare drafts of correspondence for the judge to sign. Some, however, direct their law clerks to correspond with lawyers from time to time on a variety of matters, such as inquiring about the progress of a case, scheduling a trial or hearing date, or requesting compliance with the court's procedural requirements. The judge's secretary can provide a sample of letters written or approved by the judge. The clerk should refer to these samples, or consult the secretary, for technical matters such as the form of the letter heading and opening address.

The clerk may find these general suggestions relating to court correspondence helpful:

1. Let the reader know immediately what the letter refers to. In a large law firm someone must sort the mail to see that it is delivered to the proper lawyer, and once that lawyer receives it someone must determine to which case the letter relates. You can simplify these tasks by addressing your letter to a specific lawyer rather than to a firm and by placing the case title and docket number near the top of the page.

2. Let the reader know why the clerk rather than the judge is writing. A lawyer may wonder why a law clerk is giving him instructions or requesting information. Therefore, use a simple introductory phrase such as "Judge Smith has asked me to advise you . . ." or "Judge Smith has ordered . . . ."

3. Remember that, although the letter may bear the clerk's signature, the clerk is writing on behalf of the judge. Excessive formality is not required, but undue familiarity is inappropriate.

4. Get to the subject. For example, it may be helpful to the reader to know that this is in response to a letter that the addressee wrote earlier. This can be handled simply by starting your letter, "In response to your letter of May 1, Judge Smith has asked me to advise you that matters of this kind must be raised by written motion served upon opposing counsel."

5. Remember that the clerk, like the judge, is a neutral party dealing with advocates. Unless the judge specifically di-

rects otherwise, the clerk should send copies of case-related correspondence to all counsel in the case. Even though the clerk may believe that a letter is of significance only to the addressee, the court has an obligation to avoid ex parte communications.

Official Business Envelopes

The U.S. courts pay the Postal Service for "official business" envelopes (sometimes called "franked" envelopes) at the time of printing, in addition to paying for the actual cost of the envelope. (These envelopes are sometimes referred to as "penalty mail" because of the "penalty for private use" legend they bear.) Therefore, these should be used only for mailing purposes and not for storage, hand deliveries, or other purposes. When they are used for mailing, they are to be used only for official court business, not for personal correspondence. The clerk should keep a supply of non-franked envelopes for other purposes requiring an envelope, such as hand-carried mail.

Juror Letters

Some district judges send a complimentary letter to each of the jurors after service on a given case, expressing the court's appreciation. If the judge follows this policy the office files will contain samples of letters previously sent. The jury clerk can furnish a current address list for the jurors. If the judge directs the clerk to prepare such a letter, the clerk should select a form for the letter, or compose a new one, and send a letter to each member of the jury, including alternates. If a particular juror has returned a second or third time, the clerk should make sure that the letter is different each time.

Prisoner Correspondence

Prisoners and persons who have been convicted and are awaiting sentence will frequently write district and appellate judges. Their correspondence may require special attention. The problems of a prisoner represented by a lawyer are handled the same way as those of any other litigant. If the prisoner is proceeding pro se, however, the correspondence may require special attention.

1. *Prisoner mail in general.* Prisoners write judges for a variety of reasons. Because the letters are frequently written by persons with little formal education, the clerk should be especially careful in reading the letters to try to determine whether the prisoner is requesting legal relief. For example, a letter may in substance request a reduction of sentence without clearly articulating that request. A good rule is to give the writer the benefit of the doubt and to assume that the letter requests judicial relief. If, after careful reading, the letter is still unclear, the clerk should take the matter up with the judge. Some letters ask the judge to transfer the author to another penal institution. Only the Bureau of Prisons has authority to grant this type of request. The judge may have a form letter to use in responding to such requests. If not, the clerk should prepare a letter instructing the prisoner about the procedure that must be followed, and keep an extra copy to use as a future form.

   Other letters may ask the judge for a variety of things. If it is not possible to take action on the request at once, the clerk should prepare for the judge's signature a short response to the writer acknowledging receipt of the letter.

   If the letter does not request relief that the court has the power to grant, then the judge may wish to follow this course:

   a. If the letter is from a prisoner, the reply letter should state that federal law prohibits judges from giving legal advice and suggest that the prisoner communicate with a lawyer. If the prisoner persists in writing the judge, or if the prisoner indicates financial inability to retain counsel, the judge may wish to refer the writer to an agency that regularly handles prisoner complaints or may forward the letter itself to such an agency, for example, the Staff Counsel for Inmates, Texas Department of Corrections.

   b. If the letter comes from one of the local jails, where the person is being held on a pending federal charge, and the request appears to be reasonable (i.e., "I need to get out for a few hours to make financial arrangements to keep from losing my home while I am in jail"), the judge may ask the marshal to help the person.

The clerk should *never* write anything in a letter that would give a prisoner false hopes or compromise the position of the court.

2. *Other prisoner correspondence.* Other prisoner correspondence will generally fall into one of four different categories: pleas for a reduction of sentence, requests for habeas corpus, complaints about violation of civil rights, and pleas for intercession with the Parole Commission or the Sentencing Commission.

By their nature most prisoner petitions are filed in forma pauperis. A petitioner who seeks to proceed in this fashion must obtain leave of court after filing an affidavit showing inability to pay costs. The office of the clerk of court will supply forms for this purpose. If the prisoner has some money, the court may require a modest payment, less than the usual amount of fees, to assure the petitioner's good faith.

Some pro se petitions are prepared with the assistance of law schools or legal organizations, but even when such assistance has been provided the organization will usually not provide counsel to try the case. The Criminal Justice Act, 18 U.S.C. § 3006A, permits a court to appoint compensated counsel to represent an indigent petitioner in § 2254 and § 2255 cases, though that counsel may receive substantially less than the usual fees for similar services. The pro se petitioner may file a motion for the appointment of counsel. If so, the court must decide whether the case is of sufficient likely merit and complexity to warrant appointment of counsel. The court may also appoint counsel sua sponte if it concludes that the interests of justice require it.

There is no provision for the payment of counsel in § 1983 (state action) cases or in *Bivens*-type (federal action) cases.

a. *Pleas for reduction of sentence*

(1) *Guideline-sentenced offenders.* Fed. R. Crim. P. 35(a) directs the court to correct a sentence imposed under the sentencing guidelines (see p. 60) if, on appeal, the appellate court determines that the sentence was illegal, the result of an incorrect guideline application, or an unreasonable departure from the guidelines. Fed. R. Crim. P. 35(b) authorizes the court, on motion of the government, to lower a sentence to reflect the offender's "substantial assistance in the investigation or prosecution of another" offender; the reduction is to be made in accordance with guidelines issued by the Commission pursuant to 28 U.S.C. § 994(n). The Commission has issued guidelines on this point; see Sentencing Guidelines § 5K1.1.

Except as noted below, the Rules of Criminal Procedure provide the district court no other authority to correct illegal sentences or sentences imposed in an illegal manner. However, offenders may seek the same relief by filing a habeas-corpus-type motion under 28 U.S.C. § 2255.

(2) *Pre-guideline sentenced offenders.* Fed. R. Crim. P. 35 took effect on November 1, 1987, at the same time as the sentencing guidelines. The former Rule 35 provided the court substantially greater authority to correct or reduce sentences. A statute enacted in 1987 made it clear that the old rule applies to offenders sentenced under the pre-guideline system. Because several years may elapse until the final appellate disposition of cases involving defendants sentenced prior to the effective date of the guidelines, courts may be receiving old Rule 35(b) motions for some time. Additionally, prisoners sentenced under the guidelines may nevertheless be unaware of the rule change and incorrectly seek reductions under the old rule.

Former Fed. R. Crim. P. 35 provided:

> (a) Correction of Sentence. The court may correct an illegal sentence at any time and may correct a sentence imposed in an illegal manner within the time provided herein for the reduction of sentence.
>
> (b) Reduction of Sentence. A motion to reduce a sentence may be made, or the court may reduce a sentence without motion within 120 days after the sentence is imposed or probation is revoked, or within 120 days after receipt by the court of a mandate issued upon affirmance of the judgment or dismissal of the appeal, or within 120 days after entry of any order or judgment of the Supreme Court denying review of, or having the effect of upholding a judgment of conviction or probation revocation.

If this rule were read literally, it would require the judge to make the reduction within 120 days and it would not suffice that the motion itself had been filed by then. Every circuit confronted with this issue, however, has held that it is sufficient if the plea is filed within 120 days, provided the judge acts with reasonable promptness thereafter.

If the request is in the form of a letter written by the prisoner, the clerk should:

a. Determine whether the writer seeks a reduction of sentence, and, if so, whether old Rule 35 applies and whether the request has been made in timely fashion;

b. Type MOTION FOR REDUCTION OF SENTENCE at the top of the letter if the letter does not already contain a similar caption;

c. Staple the letter and envelope together and file it with the office of the clerk of court as soon as possible, taking steps to see that the letter-motion has the court file number on the face of the letter.

After the letter-motion has been docketed and filed by the clerk's office it will be returned to the judge's chambers via the deputy court clerk. If old Rule 35(b) does not apply to the prisoner, or if the motion has not been timely filed, the judge has no authority to grant relief. If this is the case, the judge may instruct the clerk to prepare an order denying any relief and stating the reason. The clerk should find a form in the office files. If not, the clerk should prepare one to be used in the future. If a motion for reduction of sentence is filed by the defendant's lawyer, it is treated like any other motion.

If the motion has been timely filed, the clerk should write a brief memorandum stating the basis for the request and the relief sought. The clerk should attach the memorandum to the prisoner's sentencing file and give it to the judge for consideration. The judge may decide to deny relief under the discretionary authority granted by old Fed. R. Crim. P. 35(b) or to grant some form of relief. In either case, the judge may direct the clerk to prepare an appropriate order. If the clerk does not find a form in the office files, it may be helpful to prepare one for future use.

b. *Habeas corpus-like complaints*

These should be handled like a formal habeas corpus proceeding. Most district courts require the prisoner who files such a complaint to complete a special form that makes clear the complaint and the relief sought. If the prisoner–petitioner has not done so, the clerk of court should be asked to send this form to the prisoner-petitioner. The clerk of court then opens a record, as the form constitutes a petition and formally initiates a case. The letter and the form are then filed on the record.

c. *Civil rights complaints*

Requests for civil rights relief made by prisoners should be handled like other such suits. The letter should be sent to the clerk of court to open a formal record. In some courts, the complaint may be referred to a magistrate for initial examination so that, if it is found frivolous, it may be dismissed summarily without requiring even an answer. The clerk must ascertain the procedure the judge wishes to be followed.

d. *Pleas for intercession with the Parole Commission or the Sentencing Commission*

The release dates for prisoners who were not sentenced under the Sentencing Guidelines are determined by the U.S. Parole Commission. Prisoners sentenced under the guidelines may petition the Sentencing Commission to modify the guidelines used in determining their sentence on the basis of changed circumstances unrelated to the defendant, 28 U.S.C. § 994(s). Judges may receive letters from defendants asking them to intercede with either commission. The judge probably has a form letter that refers the complainant to the appropriate commission. If it appears that the letter is in effect a habeas corpus petition or civil rights complaint (e.g., if the prisoner asserts that the commission has denied him due process), it should be handled as stated above.

§ 3. Proofreading and Checking of Citations

The need for accuracy in every document issued by the court cannot be overemphasized. A document that contains misspelled words or inaccurate citations presents on its face proof of a lack of care in its final preparation. Every document must be proofread meticulously both for substantive correctness and to eliminate typographical and grammatical errors. Proofreading demands painstaking care. In checking citations the clerk must be certain that:

1. The cases cited in the opinion stand for the proposition of law for which they are cited;

2. The parties' names are spelled correctly and the volume, court, page number, and year of the decision are correctly given; and

3. The style of the citation is consistent with the style usually followed by the court.

Most judges use the Harvard "Blue Book," *A Uniform System of Citation,* as a guide. An excellent new guide is the University of Chicago *Manual of Legal Citation.*

It is good practice for a clerk other than the one responsible for an opinion to check the citations in the last draft of every opinion. A fresh pair of eyes is more likely to catch those errors that slip in from time to time no matter how carefully the judge and the clerk try to avoid them.

CHECKING AN OPINION

A clerk may be asked to review an opinion drafted by the judge. As a preliminary matter the clerk should determine that:

1. The court has jurisdiction;

2. The court's ruling, the "holding" of the opinion, is stated clearly and succinctly;

3. The facts supporting the losing party have been stated;

4. The arguments of the losing party have been stated and adequately addressed;

5. The cases cited stand for the propositions for which they are asserted; and

6. The conclusions are supported by clear reasoning and authorities.

The clerk should also seek to eliminate any errors that may have occurred in preparation. An opinion may be checked by following these steps:

1. Check the formal elements
   a. Compare the case title to the docket sheet in the clerk's office;
   b. Compare the listing of counsel who appeared in the case to the briefs and minute order or submission order in

the clerk's office (in appellate courts, this is usually done in the office of the clerk of court); and

c. If the hearing was before a multiple-judge panel, compare the judges' names and the order in which they are listed to the records of the clerk of court or the judge's notes.

2. Check all factual statements

a. Check all factual statements against the original transcripts, if any, and documents. Do not rely on factual representations in the briefs or appendix. Factual statements may be supported by citations to the original depositions, transcripts, or exhibits in the following manner: "(Smith depo., p. 10)";

b. Proofread, word for word, each direct quotation from an exhibit or a witness's testimony;

c. Be certain all omissions from quotations have been indicated by ellipses or asterisks; and

d. Verify all dates and numbers.

3. Check the accuracy of citations and of quotations.

4. Review the briefs to be certain all issues have been covered.

FINAL PROOFREADING

After an opinion has been checked and edited, the working draft will have interlineations, marginal inserts, and strikeouts and may well have been cut into pieces that have been stapled or pasted together or assembled by a word processor. Proofread the final draft to be certain that it is identical to the working draft. When a word processor is used, it is particularly easy to overlook some omission or unintended inclusion.

Proofreading of Galleys

The slip opinions of many courts are printed by commercial contract printers. Before formal publication, such printers provide the court with galley proofs that must be proofread. In those circuits for which it is the official printer, West Publishing Co. sends the slip opinions without providing galley proofs in advance. See p. 111. All proofreading is the law clerk's responsibility.

Proofreading is dull work but it is important and must be done with care and accuracy. It is most accurate when one clerk reads aloud from the copy being verified to another clerk who follows on the correct, master copy.

The reader should read all punctuation, spell out all proper nouns and foreign or technical words and phrases, and indicate whether numbers are spelled out or in figures. This technique minimizes the risk that typographical errors will be missed. Standardized proofreader's symbols can be found in most dictionaries. The use of these symbols indicates to the printer the changes that are to be made.

§ 4. Suggested Supplementary Reading

Hamley (Circuit Judge, Ninth Circuit Court of Appeals), *Sample Instructions to Law Clerks: Sample A* in *Judicial Clerkships: A Symposium on the Institution,* 26 Vand. L. Rev. 1241 (1973)

Joiner, *Operations Manual: A Modern, Efficient Use of Supporting Personnel and the Bar,* in FJC Seminars for Newly Appointed United States District Judges (1973, 1974, 1975 [c. 1976]), pp. 639–85

Law Clerks' Manual, United States Court of Appeals for the Second Circuit (August 1975)

Manual for Law Clerks and Pre-Hearing Research Attorneys, Michigan Court of Appeals (1972)

Wright, *Selection, Training, and Use of Law Clerks in United States Courts of Appeals,* 63 F.R.D. 465–88 (1974)

Appendix A
Code of Conduct for Law Clerks

CANON 1
A Law Clerk Should Uphold the Integrity and Independence
of the Judiciary and the Office

An independent and honorable judiciary is indispensable to justice in our society. A law clerk should observe high standards of conduct so that the integrity and independence of the judiciary may be preserved. The provisions of this Code should be construed and applied to further that objective. The standards of this Code shall not affect or preclude other more stringent standards required by law, by court order, or by direction of the appointing judge.

CANON 2
A Law Clerk Should Avoid Impropriety and the
Appearance of Impropriety in All Activities

A law clerk should not engage in any activities that would put into question the propriety of the law clerk's conduct in carrying out the duties of the office. A law clerk should not allow family, social, or other relationships to influence official conduct or judgment. A law clerk should not lend the prestige of the office to advance the private interests of others; nor should the law clerk convey or permit others to convey the impression that they are in a special position to influence the law clerk.

CANON 3
A Law Clerk Should Perform the Duties of the Office
Impartially and Diligently

The official duties of a law clerk take precedence over all other activities. Official duties include all the duties of the office prescribed by law, resolution of the Judicial Conference of the United States, the court in which the law clerk serves, and the appointing judge. In the performance of these duties, the following standards apply:

A. A law clerk should respect and comply with the law and should conduct himself or herself at all times in a manner that promotes public confidence in the integrity and impartiality of the judiciary and of the office.

B. A law clerk should maintain professional competence in the profession. A law clerk should be dignified, courteous, and fair to all persons with whom the law clerk deals in the law clerk's official capacity. A law clerk should diligently discharge the responsibilities of the office. A law clerk should bear in mind the obligation to treat fairly and courteously the general public as well as the legal profession.

C. The relationship between judge and law clerk is essentially a confidential one. A law clerk should abstain from public comment about a pending or impending proceeding in the court in which the law clerk serves. A law clerk should never disclose to any person any confidential information received in the course of the law clerk's duties, nor should the law clerk employ such information for personal gain. This subsection does not prohibit a law clerk from making public statements in the course of official duties to the extent authorized by the appointing judge.

D. A law clerk should inform the appointing judge of any circumstance or activity of the law clerk that might serve as a basis for disqualification of the judge, e.g., a prospective employment relation with a law firm, association of the law clerk's spouse with a law firm or litigant, etc.

CANON 4
A Law Clerk May Engage in Activities to Improve the Law, the Legal System, and the Administration of Justice

A law clerk, subject to the proper performance of official duties, may engage in the following law-related activities:

A. A law clerk may speak, write, lecture, teach, and participate in other activities concerning the law, the legal system, and the administration of justice.

B. A law clerk may serve as a member, officer, or director of an organization or governmental agency devoted to the improvement of the law, the legal system, or the administration of justice. A law clerk may assist such an organization in raising funds and may participate in their management and investment but should not personally participate in public fund-raising activities. A law clerk may make recommendations to public and private fund-granting agencies on projects and programs concerning the law, the legal profession, and the administration of justice.

CANON 5
A Law Clerk Should Regulate Extra-Official Activities to Minimize the Risk of Conflict with Official Duties

A. *Avocational Activities*. A law clerk may write, lecture, teach, and speak on nonlegal subjects and engage in the arts, sports, and other social and recreational activities, if such avocational activities do not detract from the dignity of the office or interfere with the performance of official duties.

B. *Civic and Charitable Activities*. A law clerk may participate in civic and charitable activities that do not detract from the dignity of the office or interfere with the performance of official duties. A law clerk may serve as an officer, director, trustee or nonlegal advisor of an educational, religious, charitable, fraternal, or civic organization and solicit funds for any such organization subject to the following limitations:

(1) A law clerk should not use or permit the use of the prestige of the office in the solicitation of funds.

(2) A law clerk should not solicit court personnel to contribute to or participate in any civic or charitable activity, but may call their attention to a general fund-raising campaign such as the Combined Federal Campaign and the United Way.

(3) A law clerk should not solicit funds from lawyers or persons likely to come before the court in which the law clerk serves.

C. *Financial Activities*.

(1) A law clerk should refrain from financial and business dealings that tend to detract from the dignity of the office, interfere with the proper performance of official duties, exploit the law

clerk's position, or involve the law clerk in frequent transactions with individuals likely to come in contact with the law clerk or the court in which the law clerk serves. During the clerkship, a law clerk may seek and obtain employment to commence after the completion of the clerkship; if any law firm, lawyer, or entity with whom a law clerk has been employed or is seeking or has obtained future employment appears in any matter pending before the appointing judge, the law clerk should promptly bring this fact to the attention of the appointing judge, and the extent of the law clerk's performance of duties in connection with such matter should be determined by the appointing judge.

(2) Neither a law clerk nor a member of the law clerk's family residing in the household should accept a gift, bequest, favor, or loan from any person whose interests have come or are likely to come before the court in which the law clerk serves or from any other person under circumstances that might reasonably be regarded as influencing the performance of the law clerk's official duties. A law clerk shall report the value of any gift or bequest, other than from a relative by blood or marriage, as requested by law or by the Judicial Conference of the United States.

D. *Practice of Law.* A law clerk should not practice law. A law clerk should ascertain and observe any limitations imposed by the appointing judge or the court on which the appointing judge serves concerning the practice of law by a former law clerk before the judge or the court.

CANON 6
A Law Clerk Should Regularly File Any Required Reports of Compensation Received for All Extra-Official Activities

A law clerk may receive compensation and reimbursement of expenses for all extra-official activities permitted by this Code, if the source of such payments does not influence or give the appearance of influencing the law clerk in the performance of official duties or otherwise give the appearance of impropriety, subject to the following restrictions:

A. *Compensation.* Compensation should not exceed a reasonable amount nor should it exceed that normally received by others for the same activity.

B. *Expense Reimbursement.* Expense reimbursement should be limited to the actual cost of travel, food, and lodging reasonably incurred by a law clerk and, where appropriate to the occasion, by the law clerk's spouse. Any payment in excess of such an amount is compensation.

C. *Public Reports.* A law clerk should make and file such reports as may be prescribed by law or by the Judicial Conference of the United States.

Notwithstanding the above, a law clerk shall not receive any salary, or any supplementation of salary, as compensation for official services from any source other than the Government of the United States.

CANON 7
A Law Clerk Should Refrain from Political Activity

A. *Political Activity.* A law clerk should refrain from political activity; a law clerk should not act as a leader or hold office in a political organization; a law clerk should not make speeches for or publicly endorse a political organization or candidate; a law clerk should not solicit funds for or contribute to a political organization, candidate, or event; a law clerk should not become a candidate for political or public office; a law clerk should not otherwise engage in political activities.

EFFECTIVE DATE OF COMPLIANCE

Persons to whom this Code becomes applicable should arrange their affairs as soon as reasonably possible to comply with it and should do so in any event within thirty days of the appointment.

Appendix B
Statutes Noted in Adoption of the
Code of Judicial Conduct

The report of the Conference's adoption, with modifications, of the Code of Judicial Conduct in 1973 includes the following:

In providing that the adoption of the code will not abrogate or modify any conflicting provisions of statutes or resolutions of the Conference, the Conference noted particularly the following statutes and resolutions:

Nepotism:
28 U.S.C. § 458; 18 U.S.C. § 1910; 5 U.S.C. § 3110.

Practice of Law:
28 U.S.C. § 454; 28 U.S.C. § 955; 28 U.S.C. § 632(a); 11 U.S.C. § 67(b).

Interest in Litigation:
28 U.S.C. § 455.
(But note that where the Code is more restrictive, the Code prevails.)

Conflict of Interest:
18 U.S.C. §§ 203, 205; 18 U.S.C. § 155; 18 U.S.C. § 291.

Participation in Business Corporations:
Resolution of Judicial Conference Sept. 1963 (Conf. Rept., p. 62).
Resolution of Judicial Conference March 1971 (Conf. Rept., p. 24).

Participation in Educational, Religious, Civic and Charitable Organizations:
Resolution of Judicial Conference Oct. 1971 (Conf. Rept., pp. 68, 69).

Resolution of Judicial Conference Sept. 1958 (Conf. Rept., p. 18).

Resolution of Judicial Conference, Oct. 1940:
That no secretary or law clerk should do any work outside the salary paid to him in the capacity of secretary or law clerk, or occupy or be appointed to any office in any federal or state court, including masterships, receiverships, etc., or practice law.

Financial Reporting:
Resolutions of Judicial Conference Oct. 1969 (Conf. Rept., p. 51; Mar. 1970 (Conf. Rept., p. 7); Oct. 1970 (Conf. Rept., p. 77); Mar. 1971 (Conf. Rept., p. 24); Oct. 1972 (Conf. Rept., p. 42.

Extrajudicial Service:
Resolution of Judicial Conference Oct. 1971 (Conf. Rept., pp. 68, 69).

Courtroom Photography:
Resolution of Judicial Conference Mar. 1962 (Conf. Rept., pp. 9, 10); Mar. 1965 (Conf. Rept., p. 11).

Report of the Judicial Conference, April 1973 at 11.

Notes

Notes

Notes

Notes

Notes

Notes

Notes

Notes